"While searching fo[r] universe, Andrea SkyWalk[er] batch of poems, leaving us [...] place and inspiring us to look deeper, further, and to find contentment in these turbulent times. Poems like these are restorative and show that love truly can illuminate the darkest moments."
Brandon Pitts - *TENDER IN THE AGE OF FURY* and *IN THE COMPANY OF CROWS*

"Andrea's heartfelt poetry will uplift and inspire you. I absolutely recommend this wonderful book to enjoy and share with others." Faiza Jeannie Billingsley, - *AWAKENING AS ONE PUBLISHER*

"I always enjoy the melodic movement of words and emotions across the pages when Andrea writes. You can rest assured she has felt, survived, and can testify to every thought she tries to convey! Please keep them coming!"
-Pamm Jones – *Visionary Bodhisattva,*

"Andrea writes from the depths of her soul, the center of her heart, to bring her word and truth to the world. She shares personal encounters and her reflections of life, sharing as a way for her to heal and become one with peace. Take this journey with her."
Sheri Roberts Greimes - Singer-songwriter/Musician

"The poems are a revelation to the soul. They speak to anyone who has dealt with pain, love, fear and a host of other emotions. You will laugh and cry. I recommend this book to anyone who has a love for written art."
Denise Walker-Venezia - Administrator, Delta Airlines

THE WORLD AS I SEE IT

A BOOK OF POETRY AND ART

ANDREA SKYWALKER

Additional copies can be bought at Amazon.com

Any comments can be directed to:

skywalker98270@aol.com

Copyright © 2019
Andrea SkyWalker

Produced & Printed in the United States of America
By

www.ruotto.com

THE WORLD AS I SEE IT

A BOOK OF POETRY AND ART

ANDREA SKYWALKER

TABLE OF CONTENTS

A NEW BEGINNING   1
A PLACE   2
A RARE GEM   3
A TALE OF TRUTH   4
A TIME   6
AN EXTRAORDINARY WOMAN   7
BARNACLE BILL   9
BIRDS OF DIFFERENT FEATHERS   10
BUILDING WALLS   11
CHILDREN'S GAMES   12
CONNECTION   14
COURAGE   15
CYCLE   16
DIGGING UP THE BONES   17
DO IT TODAY   18
DON'T LET ANYONE   19
DON'T THROW ME AWAY   20
DUCKIN AND DIVIN   21
EDUCATION   22
EVERYBODY WANTS TO LIVE   23
EVERYTHING CHANGES   25
EXPECTATIONS   26
FAIRYLAND   27
FIND YOUR OWN SPACE   28
FORGIVENESS   30
GIVE ME A REASON   31
GOTTA GET AWAY   32
GROW ONLY LOVE   33
HAPPINESS IS   35

TABLE OF CONTENTS cont'

I JUST WANTED A FRIEND	36
I LIKE HER THAT WAY	37
I LIKE LIGHT	38
I LIKE MEN	39
I NEVER KNEW	40
I WAS HIS WIFE	41
IF WE ALL BECOME ONE	43
I'M AWAKE	44
I'M SUPPOSED TO LIVE	45
IN THE AMERICAN DREAM	46
IT'S ALL HERE	47
JUST CALL	48
KEEP YOUR MOUTH SHUT	49
KNOCK ON MY DOOR	50
KNOWING YOU	51
LIGHTEN UP	52
LOVE	54
MUSIC	55
NEEDY	56
NEVER TOO LATE	57
NO MALE BASHING ALLOWED	58
ON YOUR JOURNEY	59
OUR PAIN	60
PICTURE IN THE MIND	61
PLEASE FIND HIM	62
POLYANNA	63
POOR ME	64
QUIET MY MIND	65
RAKE THE LEAVES	66
REBIRTH	68
REVOLUTION EVOLUTION	69
RUNNING	70
SMOOTH RIDE	71

TABLE OF CONTENTS cont'

SO EASY TO BE 72
SOMEBODY FOR EVERYBODY 73
STORIES 74
STRONGER 75
SUMMERTIME SANTA 76
TAKE ME 77
TEARS 79
THE ANCESTORS ARE CALLING 80
THE BABIES WERE CRYING 81
THE BLUE BRIDGE 82
THE BROTHERHOOD OF MAN 83
THE BUS TOUR 84
THE DREAM 85
THE FLOODGATES 86
THE GARDEN PARTY 87
THE GIRL IN THE SHOWER 88
THE MAN OF ALL MEANS 89
THE MYOHO SISTERHOOD 90
THE NATIVITY SCENE 92
THE NICEST NEIGHBOR 94
THE SAGA OF HARRY T 95
THE SEA 97
THE STORY OF MY LIFE 98
THE WHITE MAN BOWED 99
THE WOODS 100
THEY CALL IT FREEDOM 101
THOSE GOOD OLDE DAYS 102
THOSE INCREDIBLE EYES 103
THROUGH YOUR CHILDREN'S EYES 104
TIME 105
TWO WOUNDED PEOPLE 106
WAKE UP 107
WAR 108
WE ARE LIKE THE LOTUS 109

TABLE OF CONTENTS cont'

WE STAND TOGETHER	110
WE'RE READY TO FIGHT	111
WHAT IF YOU LEAVE	112
WHEN I LOOK INTO YOUR EYES	113
WHEN YOU THINK OF ME	114
WHO CARES	115
WHY HATE	116
WONDER IN THE AIR	117
WORDS	118
YOU SAID	119
YOU	120
YOU'RE STILL YOU	121

FROM THE AUTHOR

A little about my thought pattern. I like things in alphabetical order. My very first job as a teenager was as a librarian's assistant at the Ft. Lewis Army base near Tacoma, Washington, where I learned discipline and how to alphabetize. Actually, I learned discipline much earlier than that from my father, who was a drill sergeant in the army and from my mother, a very meticulous German woman. That's why you'll find every poem in alphabetical order (much to the dismay of my creative, artistic advisors). I like it that way because they're so much easier to find. That's that German sense of logic I inherited. Oh, did I tell you I'm very stubborn and don't like to follow the status quo? I've added the copyright date to each poem, so you know when I wrote it. That way you can see whether my thoughts, emotions, beliefs and opinions have or haven't changed through the years

My work spans over five decades. The first poem I remember writing, that I hung onto, was when I was fifteen. I never planned prior to 2017 to ever become a published poet. In 1999 at the age of 48 I had a major stroke. I became totally paralyzed on my right side, couldn't walk, talk or even move without assistance, much less make any rational decisions, because my brain wasn't working. I spent two months in the hospital in a wheelchair, but being the stubborn person that I am, I was determined to get back to normal, my normal. It's been twenty years now and I'm still recovering. I'm so grateful that I've come so far.

A day after the presidential election in January of 2017, I thought to myself, "I'll never make it through the next four years if I can't express myself," so I started writing poetry and haven't stopped since. That's how the book idea started. One day I was cleaning out my garage and found an old box of poetry and music I'd written 50 years ago as a teenager. Because of my stroke I lost some of my memory and had totally forgotten that I was a poet long before 2017.

Most of my poems have more than a hint of truth in them, then I might elaborate on that truth for the sake of poetic justice. Some of my earliest poetry was written during the Viet Nam War, i.e. "Cycle", "War", "Why Hate", "It's All Here", and "Children's Games". I consider them my best work and they are just as relevant today as the day I wrote them so many years ago.

Just to give you another clue about my thinking process, why would I include a meditating Santa in *"The World As I See It?"* I see Santa as a symbol accepted around the world as "the bringer of good things and joy." He flies around in the sky and brings good things and joy, on one day a year, to all the children that have been good. In my mind I see "children" as all human beings. Santa spends the year watching to see if the "children" have been good. As a Buddhist, I see Santa representing the law of cause and effect that permeates the universe. If one does good deeds, one receives a good effect. If you're a Christian, you might view Santa as representing God, who always watches over you from the sky. God is always loving and forgiving, whether you've been bad or good. In any event, however you may view Santa, he's a jolly individual who never fails to put a smile on one's face.

I hope you enjoy the book. Some of my poetry can be used as positive affirmations. I try to use simple language in my poetry with one exception, "The Myoho Sisterhood." Myoho is a Sanskrit word meaning mystic or of the mystic law. My goal is to inform, awaken, relax, and entertain. If just one of my poems can put a smile on your face, brings you a little joy, or helps you to have a good cry, then my journey toward healing is complete.

Many thanks to the owner and patrons of Cafe Zippy, the Black Lab Gallery, and the Recovery Cafe, who always welcome me and give me a platform to hone my craft. Thanks to everyone who helped me put this book together and gave me inspiration. To name a few, I'd like to thank J.J. Baker, who taught me how to use my computer, Duane Kirby Jenson and Brandon Pitts for their inspiration, encouragement, and creative advice and so many more I'd have to write another book to credit them all. Above all, I'd like to thank my editors and publisher, Mey Hasbrook and Ru Otto, without whose countless hours of trying to make sense of my non-traditional ways, and their belief in me this project would have never come to completion. I'm so lucky to have so many wonderful, loving people in my life.

After finishing the writing of the book, I decided I wanted to honor my artistic family and friends, so I included prints of some of their artwork, paintings and photography. These lovely people include Veronica Appolonia, J.J. Baker, Leslie Crusan Chapman, Cheryl Jones-Dix, Mey

Hasbrook, Dorothy Jones, Lorrie Kingsley, Ru Otto, LeSandra Vaughn,and Janie Whited.

Lastly, I'd like you to know that some of my poems have become or are being turned into songs so if you want to add to the intrigue, I suggest you try to guess which poems are already songs or which ones you think should become songs. You should also know that a second book is in the works along with an upcoming music CD. I'm the luckiest girl in the world and I love and appreciate every single one of you. Thank you so much.

A NEW BEGINNING

By Andrea SkyWalker
©2017

EVERYDAY A NEW BEGINNING
EVERY DAY A NEW START
LIFE BEGINS EACH MORNING
LIFE TEACHES US TODAY
EACH DAY FROM OUR PAST WE ARE TORN
EACH MORNING NEW CELLS ARE BORN
EACH DAY FROM YESTERDAY WE LEARN
PUT THE PAST IN A LETTER WRITTEN TO BURN
EACH DAY LIFE BEGINS ANEW
OUR YESTERDAYS ARE THROUGH
TODAY IS A NEW YOU

"Fawn" by J. J. Baker

A PLACE

By Andrea SkyWalker
©2017

LOOKIN FOR A PLACE TO HANG
A PLACE TO TWANG – A PLACE TO SANG
JUST LOOKIN FOR A PLACE

TO EXPRESS MY SELF – TO RELAX MY SELF
TO INVENT MY SELF – TO FORGET MY SELF
JUST A PLACE TO HANG

LOOKIN FOR A PLACE LIKE THIS
A PLACE I MISSED
A PLACE WHEREIN TO SHARE MY TRUTH
I'M LOOKIN FOR A PLACE LIKE YOU

A RARE GEM

By Andrea SkyWalker
©2006

NOT MANY MACHO MEN CAN CRY
NOT MANY MACHO MEN CAN ASK
WHY DID I DO WHAT I DID OR SAY WHAT I SAID
NOT MANY MACHO MEN CAN FEEL LIKE YOU DID
YOU'RE DEFINITELY A RARE GEM
A RARE GEM

NOT MANY MEN CAN GIVE AN APOLOGY
AND TAKE THE TIME TO MAKE IT A REALITY
NOT MANY MEN ARE WILLING TO DREAM
NOT MANY MEN HAVE THE CLASS THAT YOU DID
YOU'RE DEFINITELY A RARE GEM
A RARE GEM

AN APOLOGY
FOR THINGS UNDONE OR THINGS UNSAID
AN APOLOGY
NOT MANY MEN CAN WALK THEIR TALK LIKE YOU
YOU'RE DEFINITELY A RARE GEM
A RARE GEM

"Rocks" by J.J. Baker

A TALE OF TRUTH

By Andrea SkyWalker
©1984

THERE ONCE WAS A MURKY, STAGNANT,
MOUNTAIN SWAMP
WHERE NO PASSERBY WOULD STOP.
"THERE'S CERTAINLY NO BEAUTY TO BE FOUND HERE,"
THEY SAID,
AND WENT THEIR MERRY WAY.
THEN CAME THE TORRENTIAL RAINS,
WHICH SWEPT EVEN MORE MUD,
TWIGS, AND DEAD LEAVES INTO THE SWAMP,
AND THE STENCH BECAME
MORE THAN ANYONE COULD STAND.
"THERE'S CERTAINLY NO LIFE TO BE FOUND HERE,"
THEY SAID,
AND WENT ON THEIR MERRY WAY.

AS THE RAINS CONTINUED,
THE MURKY SWAMP OVERFLOWED
TO FORM A STREAM,
WHICH TRICKLED SLOWLY DOWN THE MOUNTAIN.
AT FIRST THE WATER WAS DARK AND DIRTY,
BUT AS THE SEASONS CHANGED
AND THE WINTER SNOW MELTED,
THE WATER GRADUALLY BECAME CRYSTAL CLEAR
AND THE SUN REFLECTED BRIGHTLY OFF THE SURFACE.
WILDLIFE CAME FOR MILES
TO DRINK FROM THE STREAM
AND TALL TREES BLOSSOMED
WHERE THERE ONCE WERE NONE.
EACH MORNING'S GLIMMER OF LIGHT

PEEKING THROUGH THE TREES
BROUGHT A NEW AWAKENING
TO THE SURROUNDING LIFE.

THE STREAM HAS SINCE MERGED
WITH OTHER STREAMS
TO FORM A MIGHTY FLOWING RIVER
RUSHING TO FUSE
WITH THE EVER-RIPPLING, LIFE-GIVING,
VAST AND ENDLESS SEA.
PASSERSBY NOW STOP TO MARVEL
AT THE BEAUTY OF THE RIVER,
THE SEA,
AND ALL ITS SURROUNDINGS AND WONDER
HOW IT EVER CAME TO BE.

WE MUST RETURN AGAIN AND AGAIN,
FOR THERE ARE COUNTLESS WONDERS TO BEHOLD.
AND THIS TALE OF TRUTH
MUST FOREVER BE TOLD.

"Squirrel Visit" by Andrea SkyWalker

A TIME

By Andrea SkyWalker
©2006

YOU THINK I'M SLEEPING BUT I'M NOT
I LAY AND LISTEN TO YOU BREATHE
I WAIT FOR YOU TO SMILE
BUT I KNOW IT WILL BE A WHILE SO....
I LAY AWAKE AND DREAM
OF YOUR SWEET WINE
I GET GLIMPSES OF THE TIME
THE TIME THAT YOU WERE MINE
A TIME I NEVER KNEW
THE TIME WITH YOU I SPENT
THAT WAS NEVER MEANT TO BE SO FINE
I'M HOPING TO REACH YOU
TO TEACH YOU
TO BESEECH YOU
I'M HOPING I CAN GET TO YOU IN TIME
HOW EVER IT WAS
IT MAY NEVER BE AGAIN
IT WOULD BE A WASTE TO THINK
IT COULD BE BUT THEN.....
I LAY AWAKE AND DREAM
OF YOUR SWEET WINE
AND I THINK ABOUT THE TIME
THE TIME THAT YOU WERE MINE

THE AFRO-AMERICAN MUSEUM

By Andrea SkyWalker
©2017

THE WHITE MAN'S VERSION
THE PORTRAYAL OF WHAT THEY SAY
HAPPENED IN HISTORY
TO SATISFY THE CONSCIENCE
OF THE WHITE MAN
WHO NOW OWNS THE COUNTRY

SLAVES IN A BOX
SPEAKING WITH WORDS
THE WHITE MAN FED THEM
PRAISING THEIR OWNERS

A FEW PAINTINGS
PRAISING THE CREATIVE IMAGINATION
OF THE MONKEY PEOPLE
FOR THE ENTERTAINMENT
OF THE WHITE MAN

THE AFRO-AMERICAN MUSEUM

AN EXTRAORDINARY WOMAN

By Andrea SkyWalker
©2017

A MOST EXTRAORDINARY WOMAN
THAT'S YOU
ALWAYS LEARNING SOMETHING NEW
YES
I'M AMAZED AT THE FULLNESS OF YOU
NEVER CEASES TO ENTHUSE ME
MYSTIFIES AND LEAVES ME IN A DAZE
I NEVER RUN OUT OF PRAISE
FOR A WOMAN LIKE YOU
ALL THE THINGS YOU CAN DO
I ALWAYS LEARN SOMETHING NEW
DUE TO THE FULLNESS OF YOU

"La Mujer/The Woman" by Mey Hasbrook

BARNACLE BILL

By Andrea SkyWalker
©2017

DEEP IN THE WOODS
SITTING IN THE RAIN
LOOKING FOR FOUR WALLS
OFF THE GRID - WITHOUT ANY PAIN
DYING FOR THE COUNTRY
JUST WANTING A SPRINKLE
WINDING IN A CIRCLE
WITHOUT ANY BOUNTY
GAVE UP BELIEVING
THERE'S NO RHYME OR REASON
FOR BARNACLE BILL
DONE THE DUTY
ALL I WANT IS A HOME
JUST FOUR WALLS AND A COT
IT'S NOT A LOT
BARNACLE BILL
HIDING IN THE HILLS
BARNACLE BILL

"The Hills" by Leslie Chapman

BIRDS OF DIFFERENT FEATHERS

By Andrea SkyWalker
©2016

BIRDS OF DIFFERENT FEATHERS
OFTEN GET TOGETHER
TO PARTAKE IN A DRINK OF WATER
TO QUENCH THEIR THIRST
BIRDS OF DIFFERENT FEATHERS
THEY GET TOGETHER TO DREAM
THERE'S NO JEALOUSY OR HATE
CAUSE THEY'VE REALIZED
THEY'RE ALL THE SAME
THEY'RE ALL THE SAME
BIRDS OF DIFFERENT FEATHERS
THEY GET TOGETHER FOR LOVE
THEY FLY ABOVE
THEY TAKE THE HIGHER ROAD TO LOVE
THERE'S ONLY LOVE
BIRDS OF DIFFERENT FEATHERS
THEY GET TOGETHER
FOR LOVE
THERE'S ONLY LOVE
LET US LOVE
THERE'S ONLY LOVE

"Bird" by Dorothy Jones

BUILDING WALLS

By Andrea SkyWalker
©1971

I CAME INTO THIS LONELY PLACE
HOPING TO MEET JUST ONE NEW FACE
I MET SOMEONE - BUT NOW HE'S GONE
AND ONCE AGAIN I'M ALL ALONE
THINK IT'S TIME FOR ME TO GO BACK HOME

SOMETIMES I FEEL SO SAD AND BLUE
AND WHEN I HAVE NOTHING ELSE TO DO
I SAIL INTO THE SETTING SUN
DREAMING OF WHEN I'LL MEET ANOTHER ONE
ANOTHER ONE TO BLOW MY MIND
ANOTHER ONE WHO'LL LEAVE ME BEHIND
THINK IT'S TIME TO GO BACK HOME

I'VE WAITED SO LONG
I WONDER IF THAT'S WRONG
BUT LIVING DAY BY DAY
IS SOMEONE ELSE'S THOUGHTLESS WAY
IF I CAN'T LIVE FOR TOMORROW
I DON'T WANT TO LIVE FOR TODAY

THINK IT'S TIME FOR ME TO GO BACK HOME
LIVE ALL ALONE

DO WHAT I WANT AT MY OWN PACE
FAR AWAY FROM THE HUMAN RACE

CHILDREN'S GAMES

By Andrea SkyWalker
©1969

SEE THE PLASTIC SOLDIERS CHILD
MARCHING OFF TO WAR
WITH THEIR CARBON UNIFORMS
WITH THEIR CARBON MINDS

THEY KNOW NOT WHY THEY'RE MARCHING
THEY ONLY LIVE TO DIE
THEY THINK NOT OF THEIR FAMILIES
WHO SIT AT HOME AND CRY

IT'S KILL OR BE KILLED - OR SO THEY'RE TOLD
DON'T ASK ME WHY - CHILD
DON'T ASK ME WHY

NOW SEE THE PLASTIC FAT MEN
IN THEIR SUITS AND TIES
MARCHING TO THEIR OFFICES
WHERE THEY CAN SIT AND SMILE
PUFFING ON THEIR FAT CIGARS
AND TELLING EACH OTHER LIES

LOOK AND SEE THE OTHER SIDE
THEIR SOLDIERS ARE JUST THE SAME
DON'T CRY - CHILD - THEY'RE ONLY TOYS
IT DOESN'T MATTER IF THEY'RE LAME
THEY HAVE NO NAME
THEY ONLY FOLLOW RULES AND REGULATIONS
AND PREPARE FOR THE NEXT INVASION

NOW YOU CAN PLAY THIS GAME – CHILD
DO IT AS YOU WISH –
MAKE YOUR SOLDIERS LIVE OR DIE
MAKE THEIR BLOODY BODIES TWITCH
YOU CAN ALSO BRING THEM HOME
AND SEND THE FAT MEN OFF TO WAR
THEN ALL OF A SUDDEN - CHILD
YOU'LL HAVE A WAR NO MORE

"Totem with Eagle" by Janie Whited

CONNECTION

By Andrea SkyWalker
©2017

NO NEED TO FEEL ALONE
WE'RE ALL CONNECTED
FLESH AND BONE
WHEN YOU'RE FAR FROM HOME
DON'T FEEL ALONE
CAUSE WE'RE ALL CONNECTED
NEVER ALONE
YOU'RE ALWAYS CONNECTED
TO SOMEBODY – SOMEWHERE
YOU'RE NEVER ALONE

"Swing Scene" LeSandra Vaugh

COURAGE

By Andrea SkyWalker
©2017

COURAGE - THE ABILITY
TO DIVE INTO DEEP WATER
WITHOUT KNOWING HOW TO SWIM
REGARDLESS OF THE CONSEQUENCES WITHIN

COURAGE - THE ABILITY TO JUMP

WON'T YOU JUMP WITH ME
INTO THE DEEP END
YOU WILL KNOW WHAT TO DO
THE CURRENT WILL GUIDE YOU THROUGH

CYCLE

By Andrea SkyWalker
©1969

WHEN WORLD WARS ARE OVER
AND WARRIORS TURN LOVERS
THEN SUMMER'S IN WINTER
AND SPRING IS IN FALL

OUR MINDS RUN IN CYCLES
OUR LIVES ARE LIKE SEASONS
OUR PATTERNED EXISTENCE
WE FOLLOW SO BLIND
AS RAIN DROPS OUR TEARS DROP
AS LEAVES FALL OUR MEN FALL

THE WAY THINGS ARE GOING
WE'RE NOT DUE FOR LONG
SOME CYCLES LIKE RULES
ARE MEANT TO BE BROKEN
WHEN ONE PEG IS MISSING
THERE'S NO CYCLE AT ALL

SO WARRIORS TURN LOVERS
AND THE SPELL WILL BE BROKEN
OUR NEW PARALLEL JOURNEYS
WILL LAST AN ETERNITY

DIGGIN' UP THE BONES

By Andrea SkyWalker
©2006

DIGGIN' UP THE BONES
THOSE TRIED OLD BONES
THOSE OLD BONES
THAT JUST WANT TO REST

DIGGIN' – DIGGIN' DEEPER
FOR REASONS THAT DON'T EXIST
IGNORING THAT ORDER TO CEASE AND DESIST
NOT WANTING TO BELIEVE IT'S OVER
REFUSING TO LET GO

DIGGIN' UP THE BONES
TRYING TO FIND SOME PAIN
THAT'S LONG BEEN EXPLORED
CHIPPING AWAY AT NOTHING
NOTHING'S THERE

DIGGIN' – DIGGIN' – DIGGIN'
DIGGIN' DEEP - KEEP DIGGIN'
DIGGIN' UP THE PAST
FOR WHAT I ASK
LET'S LIVE FOR TODAY

DO IT TODAY

By Andrea SkyWalker
©2017

TOMORROW'S JUST A MOMENT AWAY
A MOMENT AWAY
SO DO IT TODAY
BE ALL THAT YOU CAN BE

FOLLOW YOUR DREAMS
DON'T THROW THEM AWAY
DO IT TODAY
'CAUSE TOMORROW'S JUST A MOMENT AWAY

WHETHER YOU'RE UP OR YOU'RE DOWN
DO IT TODAY
JUST LISTEN TO ME
AND IF TOMORROW NEVER COMES

JUST DO IT TODAY
JUST DO IT TODAY

DON'T LET ANYONE

By Andrea SkyWalker
©2017

DON'T LET ANYONE TELL YOU
YOU CAN'T
DON'T LET ANYONE TELL YOU
YOU WON'T
DON'T LET THEM TELL YOU - NO
DON'T LET THEM TELL YOU - GO

DON'T LET THEM TELL YOU YOU'RE LESS
WHEN YOU FEEL LIKE MORE
DON'T LET THEM MAKE YOU FALSE
WHEN YOU KNOW YOU'RE TRUE

DON'T LET THEM HOLD YOU BACK
WHEN YOU KNOW THAT IT'S A FACT
GET READY FOR A POSITIVITY ATTACK
GO AHEAD - GO AHEAD

"Evening Preen" *by Janie Whited*

DON'T THROW ME AWAY

By Andrea SkyWalker
©2017

DON'T THROW ME AWAY
I HAVE SO MUCH TO SAY
I HAVE THINGS I CAN DO FOR YOU

JUST CAUSE I'M OLD AND GRAY
I CAN STILL DANCE AND PLAY
I CAN RUN CIRCLES AROUND THEM ALL

I HAVE SO MUCH YET TO TEACH YOU
LET ME KNOW HOW I CAN REACH YOU
YOU DON'T KNOW ME YET
AND I BESEECH YOU
DON'T THROW ME AWAY

I'M OLD ENOUGH TO KNOW
YET YOUNG ENOUGH TO LEARN
PLEASE TELL ME YOU NEED ME SO....

DON'T THROW ME AWAY
I HAVE SO MUCH TO SAY
I HAVE THINGS I CAN DO FOR YOU

DUCKIN' AND DIVIN'

By Andrea SkyWalker
©2017

I WAS DUCKIN' AND DIVIN'
AND SHUCKIN' AND JIVIN'
AND THAT'S THE WAY IT WAS
IN THOSE DAYS
THE DON'T GET TOO PERSONAL
LET'S TALK ABOUT THE WEATHER DAYS
THE HOW MUCH WOOD DID YOU CUT
FOR THE WINTER DAYS
THE HOW MANY CHICKENS
DID THE FOX GET DAYS
OOOH BUT LET'S NOT GET TOO DEEP
CAUSE THAT'S THE STUFF THAT HURTS
THAT'S THE STUFF THAT MAKES YOU CRY
AND THAT'S NOT ALLOWED
SO, I WAS ADUCKIN' AND ADIVIN'
AND ASHUCKIN' AND AJIVIN'
AND THAT'S THE WAY IT WAS

"Two Ducks" by J.J .Baker

EDUCATION

By Andrea SkyWalker
©1969

THEY SAY IT'S IMPORTANT
TO GET A GOOD EDUCATION
IN ORDER TO HAVE A VOICE
IN THIS NATION
IT'S SUPPOSED TO HELP YOU
GET A GOOD JOB
SO YOU DON'T GET TRAMPLED
BY THE MOB
IT MIGHT HELP US
FIND SOLUTIONS
TO PROBLEMS LIKE
AIR AND WATER POLLUTION
BUT SOMETIMES
IT CAN GO TOO FAR
LIKE TRYING TO PUT MEN
ON THE MOON AND MARS
IT'S BETTER TO SOLVE
SOME EARTH PROBLEMS FIRST
LIKE PEOPLE DYING OF
HUNGER AND THIRST

EVERYBODY WANTS TO LIVE

By Andrea SkyWalker
©2017

I DIG A LITTLE HERE
AND PLOW A LITTLE THERE
CAUSE EVERYBODY WANTS TO LIVE
THE DOCTOR TOLD ME TO MAKE MY WILL
I SAID, NO SIR I'M NOT READY TO GO
I STILL HAVE TOO MUCH LIVING TO DO
SO, WITH YOU I AM THROUGH
CAUSE EVERYBODY WANTS TO LIVE
YES - EVERYBODY WANTS TO LIVE

"Mountain Range" by Leslie Chapman

SO, I GO UP TO THE MOUNTAINS
WHERE THE AIR IS CLEAR
AND THE TREES ARE GREEN
OH LOOK - THERE'S A BEAR

I BATHE IN THE RIVER
AND FISH IN THE STREAM
AND I BUILD ME A CABIN
WHERE TO SIT AND DREAM
CAUSE EVERYBODY WANTS TO LIVE
YES - EVERYBODY WANTS TO LIVE

SO, THE PEOPLE IN THE CITY
THEY JUST RIP AND RUN
I TOOK A LOOK AND SAID
WELL THAT'S NO FUN
I BUILT A CAMPFIRE
AND DANCED IN THE SUN
AND THAT'S THE WAY IT'S DONE
YES - THAT'S THE WAY IT'S DONE
CAUSE EVERYBODY WANTS TO LIVE

EVERYTHING CHANGES

By Andrea SkyWalker
©2018

THEY SAY THE ONLY THING CERTAIN
ABOUT LIFE IS CHANGE
EVERYTHING CHANGES
NOTHING STAYS THE SAME

EVERYTHING CHANGES
WITH THE EVOLUTION OF THE BRAIN
EVERYTHING CHANGES
THERE'S NO NEED FOR BLAME

WINTER NEVER FAILS TO TURN INTO SPRING
CAUSE EVERYTHING CHANGES
NOTHING STAYS THE SAME

MY MIND STAYS OPEN
I WELCOME THE NEW
NEW BUDS WILL BLOSSOM
SO MANY THINGS TO LOOK FORWARD TO

EACH DAY A DIFFERENT POINT OF VIEW
CAUSE EVERYTHING CHANGES
EVERY DAY IS NEW

EXPECTATIONS

By Andrea SkyWalker
©2017

ALWAYS HAVING EXPECTATIONS
EXPECTING TO BE LIKED
EXPECTING TO BE ADMIRED
EXPECTING TO BE LOVED
EXPECTING TO BE RESPECTED
EXPECTING TO BE ADULATED

I WANT TO BE DONE WITH EXPECTATIONS
I ONLY WANT TO EXPECT TO BE ME
I ONLY WANT TO EXPECT TO BE FREE
I ONLY WANT TO EXPECT YOU TO SEE
OH WELL -
I GUESS I'M STILL FULL OF EXPECTATIONS

"Bleeding Hearts" by Ru Otto

FAIRYLAND

By Andrea SkyWalker
©2006

MUSIC - ART- GOOD FOOD
FRESH AIR AND LAUGHTER
THE HUMAN TOUCH
ALL THE THINGS THAT MEAN
SO MUCH TO ME YOU ARE

A GOOD FRIEND
SOMEONE TO TALK TO
THE NEED TO BE WANTED
HAS BEEN FULFILLED BY YOU
HUMAN KINDNESS AND DECENCY
ALL THESE THINGS YOU ARE AND MORE

A STROLL DOWN FAIRY LANE
I LOVE THE PLACE YOU ALWAYS SEND ME TO
MAY THE DUST KEEP SPRINKLING
SO I CAN STROLL THROUGH FAIRYLAND
WITH YOU FOREVER

THE WAY THINGS BEGIN
IS THE WAY THINGS END
MY FRIEND - I LOVE YOU

FIND YOUR OWN SPACE

By Andrea SkyWalker
©2006

FIND YOUR OWN SPACE
EVERYBODY'S GOT A PLACE
IN THE LIGHT OF THE SUN
YOU GOTTA FIND YOUR OWN SPACE
THERE'S ROOM FOR EACH AND EVERYONE

IN THE SUN
IN THE RAIN
UNDER THE MOONSHINE
IN SUMMER AND IN WINTERTIME

YOU GOTTA MAKE YOUR OWN SPACE
DON'T GET CAUGHT UP IN THE RAT RACE
YOU GOTTA MAKE YOUR OWN TIME
THERE'S TIME TO SATISFY YOUR MIND

"Abstract Face" by Cheryl-Jones-Dix

FORGIVENESS

By Andrea SkyWalker
©2017

PLEASE FORGIVE ME
FOR NOT BEING ABLE
TO EXPRESS MYSELF PROPERLY
AS I'VE FORGIVEN YOU
FOR NOT EXPRESSING YOURSELF PROPERLY
ONLY TIME WILL TELL
WHO WAS RIGHT
OR WHO WAS WRONG
OR WHO CARED TOO MUCH
OR NOT ENOUGH

"Snake and Statue" by Cheryl Jones-Dix

GIVE ME A REASON

By Andrea SkyWalker
©1993

GIVE ME A REASON TO BELIEVE IN YOU
I GAVE YOU ALL OF ME
AND THAT'S NOT ENOUGH
I THOUGHT IT WOULD BE
AND I WAS IN LOVE WITH YOU
THE CHOICES THAT YOU MADE
GAVE ME NO REASON TO BELIEVE IN YOU
BUT I STILL WANT TO BELIEVE
THAT SOMEWHERE INSIDE
YOU STILL LOVE ME TOO
I GAVE YOU ALL I HAD - ALL I WAS
BUT YOU WANTED MORE
THEN YOU WENT AWAY
YOU TOLD ME YOU WOULD ALWAYS STAY
WITH ME - CAN'T YOU SEE
I STILL WANT A REASON TO BELIEVE IN YOU
AND ONLY YOU
THERE IS NO OTHER
GIVE ME A REASON TO WANT TO
STILL BE WITH YOU
I WANT YOU TO BE TRUE TO ME
PLEASE GIVE ME A REASON
TO BELIEVE IN YOU - I DO
YOU TOLD ME YOU WOULD ALWAYS BE TRUE TO ME
TRUE BLUE - I'M TRUE TO YOU
YOURS TRULY - PLEASE BE MINE
MY ONE AND ONLY LOVE
LOVE YOU - I DO LOVE YOU
I DO LOVE YOU

GOTTA GET AWAY

By Andrea SkyWalker
©2017

I COULDN'T TAKE IT ANY MORE
I WAS RUNNIN IN THE DARK
GOTTA GET AWAY
GOTTA GET AWAY
LEFT THE CHILDREN BEHIND
JUST GOTTA GET AWAY - GOTTA GET AWAY
HE WON'T HURT THE BABIES
I JUST GOTTA GET AWAY
I LEFT IN THE MIDDLE OF THE NIGHT
I JUST GOTTA GET AWAY
GOTTA GET AWAY
I JUST GOTTA GET AWAY
ON THE TRAIN
THE TRAIN TO FREEDOM
I JUST GOTTA GET AWAY
SO MANY OF US
WE JUST GOTTA GET AWAY
GOTTA GET AWAY

"Migration" by Ru Otto

GROW ONLY LOVE

By Andrea SkyWalker
©2017

WHEN YOU GROW ONLY LOVE
THE WORLD BECOMES A FIELD OF ROSES
THE RED - THE WHITE
THE YELLOW AND THE BLUE

WHEN YOU GROW ONLY LOVE
WHEN YOU GROW ONLY LOVE

WHEN YOU GROW ONLY LOVE
THE AIR IS SWEET TO BREATHE

WHEN YOU GROW ONLY LOVE
WHEN YOU GROW ONLY LOVE
THE DOORS WILL OPEN ON THEIR OWN

"Pink Rose" by Leslie Chapman

WHEN YOU GROW ONLY LOVE
WHEN YOU GROW ONLY LOVE

WHEN YOU GROW ONLY LOVE
THE SUN CAN'T BE TOO BRIGHT

WHEN YOU GROW ONLY LOVE
WHEN YOU GROW ONLY LOVE

NO DAY CAN BE TOO ROUGH
WHEN YOU GROW ONLY LOVE

WHEN YOU GROW ONLY LOVE
YOU WILL GROW - YOU WILL GROW

"Essence of Iris" by Ru Otto

HAPPINESS IS

By Andrea SkyWalker
©1981

DON'T LET YOUR SMILE
TURN INTO A FROWN
DON'T LET YOUR FACE
SAG DOWN TO THE GROUND
WHENEVER YOUR PROBLEMS
START GETTING YOU DOWN
REMEMBER THERE'S SOMETHING
THAT'S THERE TO BE FOUND OUT
'CAUSE HAPPINESS IS FOR YOU AND FOR ME
IT MEANS YOU ARE CHANGING
YOUR DESTINY

PERPETUAL MOTION
WITH JUST YOUR DEVOTION
CAN SET YOUR LIFE FREE FROM
GRIEF AND FROM STRIFE
THIS IS THE RIGHT TIME
FOR ONCE IN YOUR LIFETIME
AND ISN'T IT HIGH TIME
YOU MADE UP YOUR MIND
TO DO SOMETHING WORTHWHILE
TO ADD TO YOUR LIFESTYLE
THAT BENEFITS YOU AND HUMANITY

YOU'RE SOON TO DISCOVER
THAT UNDER THAT COVER
YOU'RE REALLY THE PERSON
YOU'VE WANTED TO BE - SO....

I JUST WANTED A FRIEND

By Andrea SkyWalker
©2017

WHY DO YOU OPEN THE DOOR
THEN LEAVE ME BEGGIN' FOR MORE
I GAVE YOU ALL OF MY LOVE
ALL MY TIME - YOU WERE MINE - YOU'RE SO FINE

I LET YOU INTO MY WORLD
I GAVE YOU ALL I COULD GIVE
YOU SLIPPED AWAY IN THE NIGHT
WHILE I WAS HOLDING YOU TIGHT

I DON'T WANT YOU TO STAY ON THE OUTSIDE
WHEN I'M FEELING SO GOOD ON THE INSIDE
LIFE COULD BE THIS GOOD ALL THE TIME
IF YOU WERE MINE - I AIN'T LYIN

I'M SIGHIN - I'M CRYIN
I'M LYIN - I'M DYIN
I CAN'T DO THIS AGAIN
I JUST WANTED A FRIEND

I LIKE HER THAT WAY

By Andrea SkyWalker
©2017

SHE'S LUMPY AND BUMPY
AND SAGGY AND BAGGY
BUT I LIKE HER THAT WAY
YES - I LIKE HER THAT WAY

SHE HAS GRAY ROOTS
PUSHING OUT HER LONG BROWN HAIR
BUT I LIKE HER THAT WAY
YES - I LIKE HER THAT WAY

HE'S GOING BALD
WITH ONE TOOTH IN THE MIDDLE
BUT I LIKE HIM THAT WAY
YES - I LIKE HIM THAT WAY

HE WEARS SUSPENDERS
TO KEEP UP HIS UNDERS
BUT I LIKE HIM THAT WAY
YES I LIKE HIM THAT WAY

AND I LOVE HIM
YES - I LOVE HIM
AND I LOVE HER
YES - I LOVE HER

I LIKE LIGHT

By Andrea SkyWalker
©2017

I'M CHEERFUL IN THE SUMMERTIME
AS LONG AS THE SUN IS OUT
I LIKE TO LAY OUT AND GET A TAN
WITH CLOTHES ON OR WITHOUT
BUT AS SOON AS RAINDROPS START TO FALL
MY SPIRITS HIT THE FLOOR
I GO INSIDE MY DREARY HOUSE
STAY IN BED AND LOCK THE DOOR
SO I WENT TO SEE A THERAPIST
SHE TOLD ME NOT TO WORRY
CAUSE SUMMERTIME WILL SOON BRING BACK
THE SUNSHINE IN A HURRY
I SAID "JEE THANKS A LOT" AND PAID MY FEE
AND THEN WENT HOME AND CRIED
I THOUGHT THERE MUST BE SOMETHING I CAN DO
TO KEEP MY SPIRITS HIGH
SO, I STRUNG UP SOME SPARKLY CHRISTMAS LIGHTS
FROM THE CEILING TO THE FLOOR
THEY SENT MY SPIRITS THROUGH THE ROOF
SO I WENT OUT AND BOUGHT SOME MORE
SO NOW I KEEP THE SPARKLY LIGHTS
ON AROUND THE CLOCK
ALL WINTER - SPRING - AND FALL
I EVEN PUT SOME ON THE DOG
SHE THINKS SHE'S TEN FEET TALL
CAUSE I LIKE LIGHT
YES - I LIKE LIGHT

I LIKE MEN

By Andrea SkyWalker
©2009

I LIKE HOW THEY BREATHE
I LIKE HOW THEY SMELL
I LIKE HOW THEY DRIVE
AND NEVER REMEMBER
IMPORTANT DAYS OF YOUR LIFE
THE THINGS THEY DO SO WELL
I THINK IT'S SWELL

DAY AFTER TOMORROW
THEY MAY NOT REMEMBER YOUR NAME
BUT JUST THE SAME
I LIKE MEN

I WENT TO A CLUB AND WAS HOPING TO DANCE
KINDA HOPING I'D FIND JUST A LITTLE ROMANCE
A MINUTE TOO SOON I WAS APPROACHED BY A GIRL
I SAID JEE YOU'RE AWFULLY CUTE AND ALL
BUT OH WELL
I'LL KEEP YOUR NUMBER FOR A RAINY DAY
MAYBE TOMORROW - BUT JUST FOR TODAY
I LIKE MEN

I NEVER KNEW

By Andrea SkyWalker
©2017

I NEVER KNEW HOW STRONG I WAS
TILL I HAD TO MAKE IT ON MY OWN
WHEN I THOUGHT MY WORLD HAD ENDED
IT WAS JUST A NEW BEGINNING
IT'S NEVER THE END MY FRIEND
IT'S NEVER THE END

LIFE GOES IN CIRCLES - ROUND AND ROUND
ALWAYS LOOK UP - AND NEVER LOOK DOWN

I NEVER KNEW HOW STRONG I WAS
TILL THINKING OF YOU WAS ALL I NEEDED
TO LIFT ME UP AND KEEP ME GOING
THINKING OF YOU WAS ALL I NEEDED TO BE ME

HERE I STAND
THOUGHT I WOULD NEVER WALK AGAIN
HERE I STAND - NEVER TO FALL DOWN AGAIN
FALL DOWN AGAIN - FALL DOWN AGAIN

STRONGER AND STRONGER
AND STRONGER - AND STRONGER
AGAIN - AND AGAIN - AND AGAIN - AND AGAIN
'CAUSE FORGIVENESS SETS YOU FREE
SETS YOU FREE - SETS YOU FREE

I WAS HIS WIFE

By Andrea SkyWalker
©2017

HE WAS A GREAT MUSICIAN
AND I WAS HIS WIFE
FOR 20 YEARS THERE WAS NOTHING BUT STRIFE
WITH A FEW GOOD TIMES IN-BETWEEN
WE MARRIED TOO SOON
BARELY OUT OF OUR TEENS
HE WAS A TOP ATHLETE
SO STRONG, BLONDE AND MUSCULAR
HAD A BLACK BELT IN KARATE
AND EARNED MANY AN HONOR
ONE NIGHT I MADE HIM A GREAT DINNER
BUT LO AND BEHOLD
HE'D RUN OFF WITH A STRIPPER
AND NEVER CAME HOME
HAVEN'T SEEN HIM IN 30 YEARS
I MOVED TO THE OTHER SIDE OF THE WORLD
BUT NOTHING PREPARED ME
FOR WHAT I RECENTLY HEARD

I SAW A PICTURE OF HIM
SITTING IN A CHAIR
WITH A TUBE IN HIS MOUTH
AND A LOOK OF DISPAIR
THE NEWS OF HIS DEMISE
PIERCED ME LIKE A KNIFE
HE WAS A GREAT MUSICIAN
AND I WAS HIS WIFE

"Rock and Feather" by J.J. Baker

IF WE ALL BECOME ONE

By Andrea SkyWalker
©2017

COME TOGETHER - COME TOGETHER
IF WE ALL BECOME ONE
THERE IS NO NEED FOR WEAPONS
IF WE ALL BECOME ONE
THERE IS NO NEED FOR WAR

IF WE COME TOGETHER IN LOVE
IF WE COME TOGETHER IN LOVE

IF WE TURN "I" INTO "WE"
NOT AN "I" AND A "ME"
I LOVE AND WE LOVE
LIVE LOVE AND BE LOVE

LOVE AND GRATITUDE
LOVE AND GRATITUDE

FEED THE POSITIVE
NOT THE NEGATIVE
MAKE APPREHENSIBLE
THE ALTERNATIVE

WE'RE THE ONES WE'VE BEEN WAITING FOR
IF WE ALL BECOME ONE

I'M AWAKE

By Andrea SkyWalker
©2017

I'M AWAKE AND I'M NOT A FAKE
I HAVE BEEN AWAKENED
AND I HAVE NO NEED TO BE FAKIN' IT

I'M GONNA MAKE IT HAPPEN
AND THE CORPUSCLES ARE AZAPPIN
I'M AWAKE - YES I'M AWAKE

MAKE NO MISTAKE
YES - I'M AWAKE
I HOPE YOU CAN RELATE

THAT I'M AWAKE - YES
I'M AWAKE

TO BE ABLE TO SEE
TO BE ABLE TO HEAR
TO BE ABLE TO TOUCH
TO BE ABLE TO TASTE
TO BE ABLE TO FEEL

TO BE ABLE TO SPEAK
WHAT A BONUS

ALL THESE THINGS
I'M GRATEFUL FOR
BUT MOST OF ALL
I'M AWAKE

I'M SUPPOSED TO LIVE

By Andrea SkyWalker
©2017

I'M SUPPOSED TO LIVE
I GOT THINGS TO GIVE
I GOT PLACES TO SEE
DON'T YA KNOW
I GOT PLACES TO GO
IN WIND - RAIN - AND SNOW
AND THE CLOCK KEEPS ON TICKING
REAL SLOW

WHEN I WAS 63
I WAS TIRED AND CRANKY
AND MY PRESSURE
WAS WAY TOO HIGH
AS MY KIDNEYS WERE FAILING
AND I LAY THERE AILING
I WOKE UP AND SAID
NO- I'M NOT GONNA DIE

I'M SO LUCKY I GET A SECOND CHANCE
TO WALK AND TALK
AND LEARN HOW TO DANCE
MAYBE FIND A LITTLE ROMANCE
TO APPRECIATE EACH MOMENT AND SAY
HOW ARE YOU TODAY

LET'S TAKE A CHANCE
AND DANCE THE NIGHT AWAY
CAUSE I'M SUPPOSED TO LIVE

IN THE AMERICAN DREAM

By Andrea SkyWalker
©2017

WE START OUT FRESH AND CLEAN
IN THE AMERICAN DREAM
IN THE AMERICAN DREAM

THERE'S SO MUCH FOR ME AND YOU
IN THE AMERICAN DREAM
IN THE AMERICAN DREAM

ALWAYS SOMETHING TO DO
IN THE AMERICAN DREAM
IN THE AMERICAN DREAM

AND WE ALL GET ALONG
WE GROW BIG AND STRONG
IN THE AMERICAN DREAM
IN THE AMERICAN DREAM

THE RED - THE WHITE
AND THE BLUE
IS FOR ME AND FOR YOU
IN THE AMERICAN DREAM

AND IT ALL SEEMS SO OBSCENE
IN THE AMERICAN DREAM
IN THE AMERICAN DREAM

IT'S ALL HERE

By Andrea SkyWalker
©1969

GAPS IN GENERATION AND CREDIBILITY
FEELINGS OF HOPELESSNESS AND FUTILITY
A GENERATION MORE AWARE THAN EVER BEFORE
DEMONSTRATING BY THE SCORE
SOME PEOPLE REFUSE TO BELIEVE
THAT WARS CAN BE WON SO THEY LEAVE
OTHERS HAVE NO REASON FOR LIVING ANYWAY
SO THEY STAY
WHEN WILL OUR CITIES CEASE TO BURN
WHEN WILL THE WORLD EVER LEARN
WHEN WILL THE CHILDREN CEASE TO DIE
HOW LONG DO THEY HAVE TO CRY
HOW LONG WILL PEOPLE GO ON BURNING
PROBABLY TILL THE WORLD STOPS TURNING

"Rebirth" by Janie Whited

JUST CALL

By Andrea SkyWalker
©2017

MANY PEOPLE ARE SO ATTACHED
TO THEIR MISERY
THEY CAN'T HANDLE
ANY POSITIVITY

MANY PEOPLE
CAN'T FINISH WHAT THEY STARTED
BECAUSE THEY'RE AFRAID
AFRAID TO FAIL IF THEY TRIED

AFRAID
IF THEY MAKE A MOVE
THEY'LL END UP
WITH NOTHING AT ALL

AFRAID
THEY MIGHT BE PUSHED
AGAINST A WALL
STAND UP AND BE TALL

IF YOU'RE AFRAID
JUST CALL
I'LL BE THERE
I CARE - I SWEAR

KEEP YOUR MOUTH SHUT

By Andrea SkyWalker
©2017

JUST KEEP YOUR MOUTH SHUT
AND TRY TO FIT IN - I CAN HEAR THEM SAY
DON'T DRAW ANY ATTENTION
YOU CAN'T BELIEVE THAT WAY

THAT WAS THEN AND THIS IS NOW
YOU WON'T BELIEVE HOW MUCH
I'VE CHANGED - OH WOW

I SAY WHAT I FEEL
AND LET YOU KNOW WHAT I THINK
WON'T GET CAUGHT
ON ANYONE'S SKATING RINK

I DO WHAT I DO
AND I AM WHAT I AM
I REFUSE TO GET STUCK
WITH MY HEAD IN THE SAND

THEY TELL ME WHAT TO DO
AND WHAT I CAN'T
AND I SAY - JUST WATCH ME
CAUSE I AM

I'M GOING TO LEARN TO BE GENTLE AND KIND
I'M GOING TO LEARN TO SPEAK MY MIND
I WANT TO SEE - TO HEAR - AND TO GO
HOW FAR I GET - NOBODY KNOWS

KNOCK ON MY DOOR

By Andrea SkyWalker
©2001

KNOCK ON MY DOOR
YOU'VE BEEN HERE BEFORE
I HAVE MANY THINGS IN STORE FOR YOU
I'M SURE
JUST KNOCK ON MY DOOR
YOU WANT TO KNOW THE TRUTH
I'M SURE
THAT I'M HERE JUST FOR YOU
I'M SURE
THERE ARE PLACES TO EXPLORE WITH YOU
I'M SURE
MANY PLACES YOU'VE NEVER BEEN TO BEFORE
I'M SURE
JUST KNOCK ON MY DOOR

"Interiors" by Ru Otto

KNOWING YOU

By Andrea SkyWalker
©2001

YOUR CHARM PERMEATES MY BEING
I CAN SEE YOUR SOUL THROUGH YOUR EYES
IT IS AS DEEP AS THE SEA
AND REACHES AS HIGH AS THE STARS
I CAN SEE HEAVEN IN YOUR EYES

YOU'VE AWAKENED A PASSION IN ME
I THOUGHT WAS GONE FOREVER
YOU'VE TOUCHED MY HEART AND MY SOUL
IN WAYS YOU'LL NEVER KNOW

KNOWING YOU BRINGS ME SUCH COMFORT
BEING IN YOUR PRESENCE COMPLETES ME
THINKING OF YOU MAKES ME SMILE
AND SENDS SHIVERS DOWN MY SPINE
WHEN YOU HOLD ME I AM NOT AFRAID

ALTHOUGH MY HEART LONGS TO BE WITH YOU
MY SOUL SAYS THE TIME IS NOT RIGHT
WE BOTH HAVE THINGS WE MUST DO
I'LL BE WAITING FOR YOU
TO APPEAR ON MY DOORSTEP
TILL THEN - MY LOVE - GOOD NIGHT

LIGHTEN UP

By Andrea SkyWalker
©2017

LIGHTEN UP
LET'S TALK ABOUT IT
IT CAN'T BE ALL THAT BAD
LET'S STOP HIDING AND SHAMING EACH OTHER
AND JUST TALK ABOUT IT
LIGHTEN UP

I WANNA HEAR THAT DEEP DARK SECRET
THAT'S SO SHAMEFUL
AND TEARING YOU APART
LET'S EXAMINE IT FOR WHAT IT IS
WE'RE ALL HUMAN - I THINK

THE TRUTH SETS YOU FREE THEY SAY
FORGIVENESS IS GRACE
COMPASSION IS SO HEALING
LET'S PUT AN END TO OSTRASIZING
THOSE WE DON'T UNDERSTAND
AND ENVELOP THEM WITH INCLUSIVENESS
LOVE AND COMPASSION

ISN'T THAT WHAT WE ALL WANT
LOVE, VALIDATIION AND ACCEPTANCE
TOUCH SOMEONE'S HEART
IT'S NOT POSSIBLE TO WAGE WAR
WHILE HUGGING SOMEONE

LET'S LIGHTEN UP

WE CAN RAISE THE CONSCIOUSNESS
OF THE PLANET
IF WE JUST LIGHTEN UP

"A Cat Is A Cat Is A Cat" by Ru Otto

LOVE

By Andrea SkyWalker
©2006

LOVE MEANS
YOU DON'T HAVE TO APOLOGIZE
FOR NOT BEING PERFECT
YOU FORGIVE EACH OTHER
FOR SCREWING UP
LOVE MEANS
YOU TRUST ONE ANOTHER
WITH ALL THAT YOU HAVE
AND ALL THAT YOU ARE
LOVE MEANS
WHEN ONE FALLS DOWN
THE OTHER ONE PICKS HIM UP
LOVE MEANS
WHEN ONE IS TOO TIRED
THE OTHER ONE CARRIES THE LOAD
LOVE MEANS ONE KNOWS
WHAT THE OTHER ONE NEEDS
LOVE MEANS
THAT BECAUSE THERE IS TRUST
THERE IS NO NEED FOR LIES

MUSIC

By Andrea SkyWalker
©1967

MUSIC HAS ALWAYS BEEN A WAY THROUGH WHICH
THE WORLD CAN COMMUNICATE
ALTHOUGH BEETHOVEN IS VERY OLD-FASHIONED
PEOPLE STILL LISTEN TO HIS MUSIC WITH PASSION
EVEN THE BEATLES ARE STILL IN DATE
AND THEIR TREND OF MUSIC
IS HERE TO STAY
ALL THESE THINGS GO TO PROVE
THAT MUSIC IS IN
WHETHER OLD OR NEW

"Play My Piano" by Ru Otto

NEEDY

By Andrea SkyWalker
©2017

HUMANS ARE NEEDY
WE ALL NEED SOMETHING
NO - WE ALL NEED EVERYTHING
AND EVEN THEN THAT'S NOT ENOUGH

WILL THERE EVER BE A DAY
WHEN WE CHANGE OUR NEEDS TO WANTS
LIKE I WANT TO BE LOVED
BUT I DON'T NEED TO BE LOVED
BECAUSE LOVING MYSELF IS ENOUGH

WILL THERE EVER COME A DAY
WHEN WE DON'T NEED TO KILL
BUT WE WANT TO SAVE THE DEER - THE ELK
AND WE WANT TO SAVE THE TREES

YES - THE DAY IS HERE

NEVER TOO LATE

By Andrea SkyWalker
©2017

IT'S NEVER TOO LATE TO BEGIN
TO LOOK WITHIN AND FIND YOUR SOUL
IT'S NEVER TOO LATE
TO TRY TO BE AT PEACE

IT'S NEVER TOO LATE TO FIND YOURSELF
TO FIND THAT LIVING IS A DREAM
IT'S NEVER TOO LATE
TO FIND OUT WHY

WHY YOU GAVE UP
DOES IT REALLY MATTER
NOW'S THE TIME
TO BEGIN AGAIN

NOW'S THE TIME
TO VALUE THE MOMENT
NOW'S THE TIME TO CHOOSE LIFE
IT'S NEVER TOO LATE

IT'S NEVER TOO LATE TO BE HAPPY
TO FIND JOY
IT'S NEVER TOO LATE
TO FIND PEACE

NO MALE BASHING ALLOWED

By Andrea SkyWalker
©2009

I'M DRIFTING ON A CLOUD
NO MALE BASHING ALLOWED
I'M OPEN, FREE AND PROUD
NO MALE BASHING ALLOWED

FORGIVENESS IS GRACE
LIKE LILLIES AND LACE
I SEE IN YOUR FACE

THERE'S NO TIME TO WASTE
ON TRIVIALITIES OF THE PAST
OR TIT FOR TAT
I WON'T DO YOU LIKE THAT
SO DON'T BOTHER TO ASK

ME - WHY I DON'T REMEMBER
THE ROUGH TIMES OF SEPTEMBER
THERE'S JUICE IN THE LEAVES
AND SEEDS IN THE TREES

THERE'S JUICE IN THE LEAVES
AND SEEDS IN THE TREES
NO MALE BASHING ALLOWED

ON YOUR JOURNEY

By Andrea SkyWalker
©2006

ON YOUR JOURNEY
TOWARD YOUR SEARCH FOR YOU
I WISH YOU HOPE
I WISH YOU TRUTH
I WISH YOU LOVE

ON YOUR JOURNEY
TOWARD YOUR SEARCH FOR YOU
I WISH YOU REST
I WISH YOU PEACE

ON YOUR JOURNEY
TOWARD YOUR SEARCH FOR YOU
I WISH YOU BALANCE
WHILE WALKING ON A TIGHTROPE
AND LETTING GO TO HEAL THE PAIN

ON YOUR JOURNEY
TOWARD YOUR SEARCH FOR YOU
I WISH YOU LIGHT - I WISH YOU LAUGHTER
I WISH YOU A LUSHOUS LIFE LESS LONGING
I WISH YOU BLISS

OUR PAIN

By Andrea SkyWalker
©2001

SOME OF US WEAR OUR PAIN ON THE OUTSIDE
SOME OF US WEAR OUR PAIN ON THE INSIDE
WHERE OH WHERE DO YOU WEAR YOUR PAIN

THERE'S NO NEED FOR SHAME
THERE'S NOTHING TO GAIN OR LOSE
SO WHY CAN'T YOU SHOW YOUR PAIN
JUST LET ME EXPLAIN - YOU CAN CHOOSE

YOU CAN COME ON HOME
NO NEED TO BE ALONE
MY HEART'S NOT MADE OF STONE

IT'S ALMOST DECEMBER
A TIME TO REMEMBER
THE JOYS AND SORROWS OF LIFE
A TIME FOR CHILDREN
HUSBAND AND WIFE

LET THE MUSIC CARRY YOU THROUGH THESE DAYS
I'LL BE THERE FOR YOU TILL THE END
ON ME YOU CAN DEPEND
MY FRIEND

PICTURE IN THE MIND

By Andrea SkyWalker
©1970

PICTURE THE UNIVERSE IN YOUR MIND
THE STARS ARE ONLY MINUTE SPOTS
FLOATING THROUGH SPACE
NOW ADD ALL OF THE GASEOUS COLORS
WHICH SURROUND THOSE SPOTS
IT IS ALMOST IMPOSSIBLE TO PICTURE
ALL OF US INSIDE ONE OF THOSE SPOTS
BUT WE ARE THERE
MIGHT NOT THE UNIVERSE BE ONLY THE WOMB
OF AN INCOMPREHENSIBLY GIGANTIC CREATURE
THE STARS BEING LIVING CELLS WITHIN THE WOMB
AND WE BEING MERELY COLONIES OF BACTERIA
INFESTING A SINGLE LIVING CELL OF THE EMBRYO

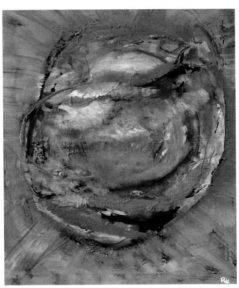

"I Am the Eggman" by Ru Otto

PLEASE FIND HIM

By Andrea SkyWalker
©2001

I WANT TO LOVE AND CHERISH THAT SOMEONE
THAT'S LOST INSIDE OF YOU
I WANT TO FIND THAT SOMEONE
THAT'S LOST INSIDE OF YOU
I WANT TO FIND AND RESCUE THAT SOMEONE
THAT'S LOST INSIDE OF YOU

BUT I KNOW I CAN'T RESCUE YOU
FROM YOURSELF ANYMORE
YOU NEED TO FIND
I REALLY HOPE YOU FIND
THAT SOMEONE
THAT'S LOST INSIDE OF YOU

I HOPE YOU FIND HIM
CAUSE I LOVE HIM
THAT SOMEONE THAT'S LOST INSIDE OF YOU
I WANT TO LOVE AND CHERISH
THAT SOMEONE THAT'S LOST INSIDE OF YOU
I HOPE YOU FIND HIM IN TIME

PLEASE TRY TO FIND HIM
I HOPE YOU REACH HIM IN TIME
THAT SOMEONE THAT I LOVE AND CHERISH
SO MUCH
THAT SOMEONE I HOPE TO TOUCH AGAIN
MY FRIEND I'M IN LOVE WITH YOU
STILL

POLYANNA

By Andrea SkyWalker
©2017

THEY CALL ME POLYANNA
CAUSE I CAN DO ANYTHING
I SET MY MIND TO

I'M A BUNDLE OF POSITIVITY
BECAUSE I HAVE A PROCLIVITY
TO BEGIN A TASK AND FINISH IT
NOT ENOUGH HOURS IN THE DAY
CAUSE EVERYTHING'S A BENEFIT

ANDA' THIS – ANDA' THAT
I KNOW WHERE IT'S AT
THERE'S NOTHING I CAN'T DO

AND YOU CAN DO ANYTHING
THAT YOU SET YOUR MIND TO
TOO

POOR ME

By Andrea SkyWalker
©2016

PO - OO - OOR ME
PO - OO - OOR ME
NO LONGER FULL OF PAIN AND MISERY
POOR ME
POOR LITTLE ME
POOR OLD ME
NO MORE EXCUSES FOR
POOR ME
FINALLY LEARNING TO JUST BE
FINALLY LEARNING TO BE ME
FINALLY LEARNING HOW TO BE FREE
NOW I SEE

"Egret and Banana Tree" by Janie Whited

QUIET MY MIND

By Andrea SkyWalker
©2017

QUIET MY MIND
DON'T OVERTHINK IT
TIME WILL BE TIME
GOOD THINGS WILL COME

QUIET MY MIND
DON'T DO IT AGAIN
ONLY TIME KNOWS
IF IT'S REALLY MEANT TO BE

QUIET MY MIND
NO NEED TO SUFFER
THINGS WILL BE REVEALED
IN THE LIGHT OF THE DAY

QUIET MY MIND
IT'S NOT A TRAGEDY
IT'S ENLIGHTENING THE NIGHT
AND BRIGHTENING THE DAY

QUIET MY MIND

RAKE THE LEAVES

By Andrea SkyWalker
©2017

TO MY CHILDREN OF ANOTHER MOTHER AND FATHER
I LOVE YOU ALL AS IF I HAD BIRTHED YOU MYSELF
MY WOMB IS BARREN BUT MY HEART IS NOT
IN MY HEART I HAVE ROOM FOR ALL OF YOU

I WASN'T THERE TO WIPE THOSE SNOTTY NOSES
AND CHANGE THOSE SOILED DIAPERS
BUT I WOULD HAVE IF I COULD HAVE

I WASN'T THERE WHEN YOU SKINNED YOUR KNEE
I WOULD HAVE KISSED IT TO MAKE IT ALL BETTER

I WASN'T THERE TO SUMMON THE TOOTH FAIRY
WHEN YOU PUT ONE UNDER THE PILLOW
BUT I WOULD HAVE IF I COULD HAVE

I WASN'T THERE TO MAKE YOU LUNCH
BEFORE YOU LEFT FOR SCHOOL
BUT I WOULD HAVE IF I COULD HAVE

I WASN'T THERE TO HUG YOU
WHEN YOU LOST YOUR FIRST LOVE
BUT I WOULD HAVE IF I COULD HAVE

MOST OF YOU NOW HAVE KIDS OF YOUR OWN
WITH SNOTTY NOSES AND SOILED DIAPERS
AND I LOVE THEM ALL TOO

I'M HERE NOW WITH LOTS OF TIME
AND LOVE TO GIVE YOU ALL
I'M HERE NOW TO MAKE IT ALL BETTER
HOPE IT'S NOT TOO LATE FOR A HUG AND A SQUEEZE

EACH OF YOU I LOVE AND BLESS
ALL I ASK IS THAT YOU RAKE THE LEAVES
AND DON'T LEAVE A MESS
YOURS TRULY - ONE OF YOUR MOTHERS

"Leaves" by J.J. Baker

REBIRTH

By Andrea SkyWalker
©2017

I'M WITNESSING A BIRTH
A REBIRTH
THE BEGINNING OF SOMETHING NEW
JUST PUT ASIDE THE OLD

LEARN FROM IT - LEARN
THE AMNIOSYNTHESIS
THE EVOLUTION OF MANKIND

WE'RE MOVING FORWARD
BACKWARD
AND ALL AROUND

EVERYDAY IS NEW
A NEW ME - A NEW YOU

"Chanterelles" by Leslie Chapman

REVOLUTION EVOLUTION

By Andrea SkyWalker
©2017

IN THESE TRYING TIMES
WE ARE WITNESSING HISTORY BEING MADE
THIS IS JUST THE BEGINNING
OF THE EARTH COMING TOGETHER

IN THIS TIME OF NEED
A PEOPLE'S REVOLUTION
A HUMAN REVOLUTION
THE BEGINNING
OF THE TRUE BROTHERHOOD OF MAN

THE COMING OF THE NEW EARTH
THIS IS THE START OF A NEW BEGINNING
OF BROTHERLY LOVE
THE BEGINNING OF A NEW WORLD
BASED ON LOVE - CARE - AND SELFLESSNESS

A NEW HUMANITY IS EMERGING
FROM THE FUNDAMENTAL DARKNESS
A NEW AWAKENING
THE POWERLESS ARE THE MOST POWERFUL
HUMANITY IS ON THE FRONT LINES
OF REVOLUTIONARY LOVE

RUNNING

By Andrea SkyWalker
©2017

I'M IN EUROPE
RUNNING FOR THE MOUNTAINS
WHILE THE FURER SPEAKS
HE SPEAKS
OF MAKING THE COUNTRY GREAT
WHILE I'M WAITING
FOR THE BLITZKRIEG TO BE OVER
SO I CAN ONCE AGAIN
SEE MY BEAUTIFUL HOMELAND

"Full Moon Mountains" J.J. Baker

SMOOTH RIDE

By Andrea SkyWalker
©2017

MY OLD FRIEND
YOU'RE SUCH A SMOOTH RIDE
A SMOOTH RIDE I SAID

WITH YOUR HEADLIGHTS BULGING
AND YOUR TAILLIGHTS BLINKING
AND YOUR BODY SO LONG AND SMOOTH
NEVER A COUGH OR A SPUTTER OR A SNEEZE
YOU HAVE A CLEAN BILL OF HEALTH
AFTER ALL THESE YEARS

MY OLD FRIEND
WHEN I CLIMB INTO YOU
WHEN I SIT IN YOUR LAP OF LUXURY
I FEEL SO LOVED AND SAFE

YOU OFTEN TAKE ME CLIMBING
TO THE HILLTOP
OR DOWN ON THE PLAIN
OR TO THE WATER'S EDGE

WHEN PARTING YOU GIVE ME A WINK
I CAN'T WAIT UNTIL TOMORROW
WHEN I CAN CRUISE
INTO THE SUNSET WITH YOU

SO EASY TO BE

By Andrea SkyWalker
©1970

I WAS WALKING HOME ONE DAY
WHEN A CAT LEAD ME ASTRAY
AND I NEVER MADE IT HOME
THAT'S WHEN I BEGAN TO ROAM

I'VE BEEN GONE A LONG, LONG TIME
AND THERE'S NOT MUCH THAT IS MINE
BUT I'VE LEARNED A LOT OF LIFE
AND I'M GLAD TO BE ALIVE

GUESS I'LL GO AND SEE MY MOTHER
SAY HELLO TO LITTLE BROTHER
THEN I'LL JUST BE ON MY WAY
MAYBE I'LL BE BACK SOMEDAY

SOMEBODY FOR EVERYBODY

By Andrea SkyWalker
©2001

THERE'S SOMEBODY FOR EVERYBODY TO LOVE
THERE'S SOMEBODY FOR EVERYBODY TO HUG
HOLD THEM IN THE LIGHT OF YOUR EYES
DANCE WITH EVERY BEAT OF YOUR HEART
HOLD THEM IN YOUR ARMS AND LET THEM KNOW
THAT THEY'RE A PART OF YOUR LIFE

THERE'S SOMEBODY FOR EVERYBODY TO LOVE
AND YOU'RE THE ONE
I SPEND ALL MY TIME THINKING OF
HOLD ME IN THE LIGHT OF YOUR EYES
LET'S DANCE WITH EVERY BEAT OF OUR HEARTS
HOLD ME IN YOUR ARMS AND LET ME KNOW
THAT I'M A PART OF YOUR LIFE

THERE'S SOMEBODY FOR EVERYBODY TO LOVE
AND YOU'RE THE ONE
I SPEND ALL MY TIME THINKING OF
HOLD ME IN THE LIGHT OF YOUR EYES
LET'S DANCE WITH EVERY BEAT OF OUR HEARTS
THERE'S SOMEBODY FOR EVERYBODY TO LOVE

STORIES

By Andrea SkyWalker
©2017

I'M QUIETLY LISTENING
TO THE STORIES
BEING TOLD
EVERYBODY'S GOT
A STORY
THE HAPPY STORIES
THE SAD STORIES
WHAT'S YOUR STORY

"Mystical Dawn" by Janie Whited

STRONGER

By Andrea SkyWalker
©2017

I AM STRONGER THAN EVER BEFORE
I WILL BE STRONGER FOREVER MORE

MY BODY GROWS OLD AND WEAK
BUT MY MIND AND HEART ARE STRONG
FORTUNATELY MY INNATE WISDOM
HAS BROUGHT ME ALONG

THE SOFTNESS OF MY BONES IS NO MATCH
FOR MY DETERMINATION
AND THE SOFTNESS OF MY HEART
HAS STRENGTHENED MY SPIRIT
AND AT TIMES GIVEN ME ELATION

WON'T YOU JOIN ME
IN THE PROCESS OF LIVING
WON'T YOU JOIN ME
IN THE PROCESS OF LOVE

SUMMERTIME SANTA

By Andrea SkyWalker
©2017

WE WENT FOR A DRIVE TO THE COUNTRY
ONE HOT SUMMER DAY
WHEN LO AND BEHOLD
THERE WAS SANTA ON HIS SLEIGH
HE HAD PLUMS AND APPLE TREES
AS FAR AS THE EYE COULD SEE
AND THE SUGAR PLUM FAIRIES
WERE PICKING WITH GLEE
TO BRING TO THE CHILDREN
BACK IN THE CITY
THE REINDEER WERE GRAZING
ON CAULIFLOWER LEAVES
WHILE THE RABBITS WERE DIGGING UP
THE CARROTS WITH EASE
HE BID US GOODBYE AND SAID
COME BACK AND REMEMBER
THE WINTER SQUASH WILL BE
READY IN DECEMBER
HE WAS PLOWING THE FIELDS
AND BAILING THE HAY AND SAID
PLEASE COME BACK AGAIN ONE DAY
HE'S SUMMERTIME SANTA

"Meditating Santa" by Lorrie Kingsley

TAKE ME

By Andrea SkyWalker
©2006

YOU CAN TAKE ME IN A BOAT
YOU CAN TAKE ME ON A PLANE
YOU CAN TAKE ME ANYWHERE
IN YOUR LIMOUSINE
JUST TAKE ME
ALL YOU GOTTA DO IS JUST TAKE ME
YOU DON'T NEED TO EXPLAIN
ALL YOU GOTTA DO IS TAKE ME THERE

YOU CAN TAKE ME ON A BIKE
YOU CAN TAKE ME ON A BUS
I DON'T CARE IF THEY STARE
AND TALK ABOUT US
JUST TAKE ME - HEAR WHAT I SAY
JUST TAKE ME
THERE'S NO NEED TO EXPLAIN
ALL YOU GOTTA DO IS TAKE ME THERE

ALL YOU GOTTA DO IS KISS
JUST KISS AND HOLD ME TIGHT
YOU DON'T NEED TO LIFT ME UP
LIFT ME UP WITH ALL YOUR MIGHT
I'LL BE YOUR CHERRY JUBILEE
IN THE MIDDLE OF THE NIGHT
JUST TAKE ME THERE
AND DO IT RIGHT

JUST TAKE ME
ALL YOU GOTTA DO IS JUST TAKE ME
YOU DON'T NEED TO EXPLAIN
ALL YOU GOTTA DO IS TAKE ME THERE

"Highway to Paradise" by Ru Otto

TEARS

By Andrea SkyWalker
©2017

TEARS ARE GOOD
THEY CLEANSE THE SPIRIT
TEARS ARE HEALTHY
THEY CLEANSE THE SOUL
TEARS REVEAL THE HIDDEN HEARTACHE
TEARS REVEAL THE JOY AND PAIN
TEARS ARE LIKE A DROP OF RAIN
T –E– A – R – S
T –E– A – R – S

THE RAIN WASHES AWAY THE SORROW
AND ALLOWS YOU TO GROW
T –E– A – R – S
T –E– A – R – S

MY TEARS ARE HERE FOR YOU
T –E– A – R – S
T –E– A – R – S

THE ANCESTORS ARE CALLING

By Andrea SkyWalker
©2017

I CAN HEAR THE ANCESTORS CALLING
CALLING US TO CARRY ON THE OLD WAYS
CALLING US TO FIND TRUTH AND HARMONY
CALLING US TO SING AND DANCE
AND FIND ROMANCE
THE ANCESTORS ARE CALLING
THEY'RE CALLING US TO FIND A WAY
TO GET ALONG
TO LOVE AND HONOR EACH OTHER
TO CHERISH AND KEEP EACH OTHER'S SPIRIT SAFE
THE ANCESTORS SURROUND US WITH LOVE

"Ancestors" by Cheryl Jones-Dix

THE BABIES WERE CRYING

By Andrea SkyWalker
©2017

AS I WAS FLYING
FROM THE EAST COAST
TO THE WEST COAST
THE BABIES WERE CRYING
FOR MILK AND HONEY
WHILE THE SCHNAUSER
WAS BARKING
THE GERMAN SCHNAUSER
AND I WAS WRITING
IN THE DARK

"Dawn Flight" by Janie Whited

THE BLUE BRIDGE

By Andrea SkyWalker
©2017

I'M AFRAID TO TRAVEL
ON THE BLUE BRIDGE TO NOWHERE
WHERE IS EVERYONE GOING
ON THE BLUE BRIDGE TO NOWHERE
OOOOH
I'M RIGHT NEXT TO
THE BLUE BRIDGE TO NOWHERE
BUT I WON'T GET ON
THEY ALL HUSTLE AND BUSTLE
TO NOWHERESVILLE
AND I REFUSE TO JOIN THEM
ON THE BLUE BRIDGE TO NOWHERE

"Hood Canal" by Janie Whited

THE BROTHERHOOD OF MAN

By Andrea SkyWalker
©2001

HOW CAN I KNOW THE BROTHERHOOD OF MAN
IF I'VE NEVER BEEN A BROTHER
HOW CAN I SEE THE BROTHERHOOD OF MAN
IF WE'VE NEVER SEEN EACH OTHER
HOW CAN I KNOW YOU - IF I DON'T KNOW ME

HOW CAN I SAY WHAT I WANT YOU TO BE
IF I HAVE NEVER BEEN
HOW CAN I KNOW WHAT YOU ARE TO ME
IF YOU'VE NEVER BEEN FREE
HOW CAN I BE ME - IF YOU CAN'T BE YOU

I NEED YOU TO HEAR AND I NEED YOU TO FEEL
WHAT IT MEANS TO BE REAL
HOW WILL YOU KNOW WHAT IT MEANS TO BE TRUE
IF THERE'S NOT A ME AND YOU
HOW CAN YOU BE ME - IF I CAN'T BE YOU

THE BUS TOUR

By Andrea SkyWalker
©2017

LOOKING THROUGH SCREENED WINDOWS
IN 95 DEGREE SWELTERING HEAT
AT THE SITES OF THE CITY
WHERE ARE THE STATUES
HONORING THE PEOPLE
WHO REALLY BUILT THIS COUNTRY
WHERE WAS THE AIR CONDITIONING
FOR THE PEOPLE WHO SLAVED
FROM DAWN TILL DUSK
TO MAKE THIS COUNTRY GREAT
WHERE ARE THE STATUES
TO HONOR THE PEOPLE
WHO SACRIFICED THEIR LIVES
TO MAKE THIS COUNTRY WHAT IT IS
WHO PICK UP THE TRASH
ON THE STREETS BETWEEN
THE HISTORIC BUILDINGS
THE TOURISTS PAY GREATLY TO SEE
WHERE OH WHERE IS THE TRUTH?

THE DREAM

By Andrea SkyWalker
©2017

YOU ARE WHAT YOU DREAM
AND I DREAM OF PEACE
YOU ARE WHAT YOU DREAM
AND I DREAM OF LOVE
YOU ARE WHAT YOU DREAM
AND I DREAM OF UNITY
YOU ARE WHAT YOU DREAM
AND I DREAM OF MUSIC AND POETRY
YOU ARE WHAT YOU DREAM
AND I DREAM OF SACRED WATER

SACRED WATER - SACRED WATER
SACRED WATER - SACRED WATER
SACRED WATER - SACRED WATER
SACRED WATER - SACRED WATER

"The Sea" by J.J.Baker

THE FLOODGATE

By Andrea SkyWalker
©2006

THE FLOODGATE OPENED
AND LOVE CAME POURING OUT
GONE WERE THE DARK DAYS
GONE WAS CONFUSION
GONE WAS THE FEAR AND DOUBT

THE FLOODGATE OPENED
AND OUT CAME LOVE
GONE WAS THE JUDGMENT
GONE WAS THE WONDERING WHY

IN CAME THE GOODNESS
IN CAME THE LIGHT
IN CAME THE HEALING
IN CAME THE FULLNESS OF YOU

THE GARDEN PARTY

By Andrea SkyWalker

©2017

NINE ETHERIC ANGELS CAME FROM ALL REALMS
BEARING GIFTS IN EUROPEAN PORCELAIN
WHILE BIRDS OF PARADISE
HUMMED IN THE TREES ALL AFTERNOON
THE SUN SHONE BRIGHTLY ON US ALL
WHILE THE WATERS OF LIFE
WERE READILY AVAILABLE
TO SOOTHE THE SOUL
ALL OF LIFE CHEERED US ON IN THE BACKGOUND
WHILE THE WILD ONES - NORMALLY ENEMIES
COURTED EACH OTHER
OTHERS CAME TO OBSERVE WITH CURIOUS EYES
NINE ETHERIC ANGELS DRIFTED AWAY
AS QUICKLY AS THEY APPEARED
WHILE THE FULL MOON ROSE
IN THE EVENING SKY
AND THE MEMORY OF A GOOD TIME
WAS HAD BY ALL

"Spring Fling" by Ru Otto

THE GIRL IN THE SHOWER

By Andrea SkyWalker
©2017

THERE WAS A YOUNG GIRL IN THE SHOWER
SHE WOULDN'T STOP TALKING
I FINALLY SAID
YOU SHOULD HAVE BEEN A TV REPORTER
BECAUSE YOU ASK SO MANY QUESTIONS
VERY INTELLIGENT QUESTIONS
I MIGHT AD
SHE SAID NO - I WANT TO BE A LAWYER
SO I KEPT LISTENING
I LEARNED SO MUCH
FROM THIS INTELLIGENT YOUNG GIRL
HOW ELSE DO YOU FIND THINGS OUT
IF YOU DON'T ASK QUESTIONS
SO I'LL ALWAYS REMEMBER
THE GIRL IN THE SHOWER

THE MAN OF ALL MEANS

By Andrea SkyWalker
©2006

HE'S A MYSTERY TO ME
THE MAN OF ALL MEANS
NEVER COMING - NEVER GOING
HE'S THE MAN OF ALL MEANS
YOU THINK ALL. - YOU SAY ALL
YOU DO ALL - YOU KNOW ALL
YOU'RE THE MAN OF ALL MEANS
HE'S NEVER IN JEANS
THIS MAN OF ALL MEANS
ONLY A TUX WILL DO
AND ALWAYS SOMETHING NEW
HE NEVER GETS BORED
HAS A TENDENCY TO HOARD
WORKS EXQUISITELY TOWARD
SOME KIND OF INTRIGUE
HE CARRIES A GUN - NOT INTENDING TO USE IT
HIS TONGUE'S A SHARP ENOUGH SWORD
HIS ECCENTRIC ENDEAVORS
ARE EXCEEDINGLY CLEVER
WITH THE MAN OF ALL MEANS
IT ALWAYS GETS BETTER
FOR THE MAN OF ALL SEASONS
THERE'S ALWAYS A REASON
AND ALWAYS A NEW PLAN
THAT HE'S SEARCHING FOR
HIS ECCENTRIC ENDEAVORS
ARE EXCEEDINGLY CLEVER
WITH THE MAN OF ALL MEANS
IT ALWAYS GETS BETTER

THE MYOHO SISTERHOOD

By Andrea SkyWalker
©2005

AS WE PRAY EACH TOGETHER
WE'RE THE MYOHO SISTERHOOD
WE'VE BEGUN A MOST PEACEFUL REVOLUTION
NOW'S THE TIME - IT'S DIVINE
WE ARE SHINY AND NEW
IT IS TIME TO HELP ONE ANOTHER

AS WE RISE WITH THE SUN
WE'RE THE MYOHO SISTERHOOD
BEING DIFFERENT - YET STILL THE SAME
EACH UNITING WE PRAY FOR SECURITY
LIVING HERE IN THE RED, WHITE, AND BLUE

AS WE STAND EACH TOGETHER
WE'RE THE MYOHO SISTERHOOD
EACH WILL TEACH THE ONE
WHO CAME BEFORE
NO MORE FEAR - VICTORY'S HERE
WE ARE HAPPY AND FREE
WE ARE EACH HERE TO SAVE ETERNITY

AS WE EACH COME TOGETHER
WE'RE THE MYOHO SISTERHOOD
WE SEEK PEACE AND HARMONY
PLEASE DON'T HIDE - LOOK INSIDE
THERE'S A TREASURE INDEED
LET THE LOTUS BLOOM AND SEED

AS WE PRAY EACH TOGETHER
WE'RE THE MYOHO SISTERHOOD
WE'VE BEGUN A MOST PEACEFUL REVOLUTION

"Myoho Sisterhood" by Ru Otto

THE NATIVITY SCENE

By Andrea SkyWalker

©2017

I STILL REMEMBER THE DAY WHEN AT EIGHT
I STARRED IN THE CHURCH'S NATIVITY PLAY
I MADE PLENTY OF SNOWBALLS THAT DAY
AND I COULD HEAR THE CHOIR SINGING
IT WAS CHRISTMAS EVE
AND THE CHURCH BELLS WERE RINGING

MY DAD WAS VISITING FOR CHRISTMAS FROM KOREA
HE WORKED FOR UNCLE SAM
KEEPING OUR COUNTRY SAFE FROM HARM
WHILE THE REST OF US STAYED HOME ON THE FARM
SO TO THE CHURCH WE WALKED HAND IN HAND
THROUGH THE BLIZZARDING SNOWSTORM
MY MOM SAT IN THE FRONT ROW
LOOKING SO PROUD
BUT WHERE'S MY DAD –?
HE WAS NOWHERE TO BE FOUND
WHEN THE PLAY WAS OVER
AND I WAS BEAMING WITH PRIDE
I SAID WHERE'S DAD - SHE SAID HE'S COLORED
SO HE HAD TO WAIT OUTSIDE

WHILE WE WERE INSIDE PRAISING THE LORD
HE WAS OUTSIDE IN THE COLD - STIFF AS A BOARD
SOMETHING CHANGED INSIDE ME THAT DAY
AND I BEGAN MY SEARCH FOR ANOTHER WAY

THAT'S WHEN I LEARNED
AT THE AGE OF EIGHT
THAT WE ARE NOT ALL EQUAL
BUT LET ME GET THIS STRAIGHT
THE STORY'S NOT OVER- OH NO

PLEASE STAY TUNED FOR THE SEQUEL – AHO

"Snow Country" by Dorothy Jones

THE NICEST NEIGHBOR

By Andrea SkyWalker
©2017

I HAVE THE NICEST NEIGHBOR IN THE WORLD
WHEN I'M GONE SHE WATCHES MY BACK
SHE EVEN FEEDS MY CAT
SHE TAKES IN MY MAIL
IF ANYONE TRIES TO BREAK IN
THEY'RE GOING TO JAIL
DON'T MESS WITH HER
CAUSE SHE'S THE REAL DEAL
SHE HELPS ANYONE IN NEED
SHE EVEN PULLS MY WEEDS
WE DON'T HAVE TO TALK EVERYDAY
BUT WE KEEP EACH OTHER SAFE
THE WORLD WOULD BE A BETTER PLACE
IF THEY HAD A NEIGHBOR LIKE HER
SHE'S FULL OF GRACE

THE SAGA OF HARRY T

By Andrea SkyWalker
©1980

IT WAS MAY OF 1980 WHEN ME
AND THE WIFE WENT TO SEE OLD HARRY T
HE WAS PROUD AND FREE AS ANY MAN COULD BE
AND THE EARTH WAS SHAKING BENEATH OUR FEET
AS WE WENT UP TO GREET OLD HARRY T

WE TOLD HIM THAT HE'D BETTER MOVE ON - BUT HE
SAID,
"I'VE BEEN ON THIS DAMN MOUNTAIN TOO LONG.
I MAY BE OLD BUT THAT DOESN'T MEAN
I AIN'T STRONG.
WELL IT'S GETTING LATE AND I HAVEN'T ATE,"
AND THEN HE BEGAN TO LAUGH
HE TOLD ME HIS STORY
THEN IN ALL OF HIS GLORY SAID,
"PUT THIS ON MY EPITAPH".....
MY NAME IS HARRY T. AND I'M 83
I'M AS ORNERY AS ANY MAN COULD BE
THEY SAY THIS MOUNTAIN'S GONNA BLOW
BUT I AIN'T GONNA GO
IF THAT'S THE WAY IT'LL BE
THEN IT'LL HAVE TO TAKE ME"

AND SURE ENOUGH IT WENT OFF WITH A SOUND
THAT WAS HEARD FOR 300 MILES AROUND
SOME LIVES WERE LOST BUT THE GREATEST
DEVASTATION
WAS TO THE TREES AND VEGETATION
WHICH CAME DOWN IN A GREAT WALL OF MUD

THAT CAUSED THE WHOLE COUNTRYSIDE TO FLOOD
ONE OF THE BODIES THAT WAS NEVER RECOVERED
WAS HARRY'S - HE WAS A STUBBORN OLD BUZZARD
AND TO THIS DAY I CAN HEAR HIM SAY....

*"MY NAME IS HARRY T AND I'M 83
I'M AS ORNERY AS ANY MAN COULD BE
THEY SAY THIS MOUNTAIN'S GONNA BLOW
BUT I AIN'T GONNA GO
IF THAT'S THE WAY IT'LL BE
THEN IT'LL HAVE TO TAKE ME"*

ASHES TO ASHES - DUST TO DUST
HE WAS A REAL TRU - MAN

"Trees" by Cheryl Jones Dix

THE SEA

By Andrea SkyWalker
©2017

THE ETERNITY OF THE SEA IS ENDLESS
EACH GRAIN OF SAND ON THE BEACH
CARRIES THE STORIES
OF THE UNIVERSE WITHIN IT
THE TIDE BRINGS IN THE OLD
AND THE NEW
THE KNOWLEDGE IN JUST ONE ROCK
WOULD MAKE YOUR HEAD SPIN
WHAT COMES THEN GOES
ONLY TO RETURN AGAIN
SUCH IS THE SEA

"Ocean/Cliff/Waves" by Dorothy Jones

THE STORY OF MY LIFE

By Andrea SkyWalker
©2006

IT'S THE STORY OF MY LIFE
I'M ALWAYS WAITING FOR SOMEONE
TO COME HOME TO ME
JUST CRYING AND WAITING FOR SOMEONE
TO COME HOME TO ME
I'M GROWING TIRED OF WAITING FOR SOMEONE
TO COME HOME TO ME
I'M GROWING OLD JUST WAITING FOR SOMEONE
TO COME HOME TO ME
THERE WAS A TIME I NEEDED NO ONE
I WAS HAPPY BEING ALONE WITH ME
NOW I'M DYING A LITTLE MORE EACH DAY
WHILE I'M WAITING FOR THAT SOMEONE
I'M JUST WAITING FOR THAT SPECIAL SOMEONE
TO COME HOME TO ME

THE WHITE MAN BOWED

By Andrea SkyWalker
©2017

AND THE WHITE MAN BOWED
TO THE INDIAN MAN
HE SAID I'LL HONOR YOUR TREATIES
AND GIVE YOU YOUR LAND

HE SAID IT'S TIME TO PUT
ALL THAT HISTORY BEHIND US
AND PLEASE FORGIVE US
WE WERE SO BLIND

BLIND TO THE BEAUTY OF THE PEOPLE
AND THE BEAUTY OF THE LAND
LET'S GIVE EACH OTHER A HELPING HAND

CAN WE LEARN TO SHARE
CAN WE MAKE IT SQUARE
IF YOU DARE
WE CAN BOTH BE HAPPY IF WE CARE

LET'S PUT OUR DIFFERENCES ASIDE
AND LOVE THIS COUNTRY FAR AND WIDE
ACROSS THE LAND
WE'RE THE BROTHERHOOD OF MAN

BE ALL THAT YOU CAN BE
A DOCTOR - LAWYER - INDIAN CHIEF
LET US TRY SOME MUTUAL RESPECT
I HAVE A FEELING
YOU AIN'T SEEN NOTHIN YET

THE WOODS

By Andrea SkyWalker
©2017

THE WOODS CAN BE A DARK, SCARY PLACE
WHERE YOU GO TO FACE THE DRAMA
THE TRIALS AND TRIBULATIONS
THE SUCESSES AND FAILURES
THE LOVES AND LOSSES
THE BIRTHS AND DEATHS
OF BELOVED FRIENDS AND PETS

OR - THE WOODS CAN BE PLEASANT PLACE
TO GET AWAY FROM THE HUMAN RACE
A PLACE TO GET SOME FRESH AIR
PROVIDED BY LIFEGIVING EVERGREENS
TO ENJOY THE SITES AND SOUNDS
OF ANIMALS WHO ONLY LIVE IN PEACE
I CHOOSE TO LOVE THE WOODS

"Tree with Roots" by Mey Hasbrook

THEY CALL IT FREEDOM

By Andrea SkyWalker
©1968

WELL YOU GO TO SCHOOL
TILL YOUR ALMOST GROWN
AND THEN THEY TAKE YOU
AWAY FROM HOME
THEY MAKE YOU FIGHT IN A WAR
YOU DON'T BELIEVE IN
YOU'RE FORCED TO KILL THE PEOPLE
WHO ONLY WANT THEIR FREEDOM
THEY TELL YOU YOU'RE ONLY
FIGHTING FOR DEMOCRACY
BUT FORCING IT ON SOMEONE IS
WHAT YOU CAN'T SEE
ONE PATRIOT ASKS
WHAT WOULD YOU RATHER BE
A COMMUNIST OR FREE LIKE ME
FREE TO DO WHAT YOU ASK
AS YOU THINK ABOUT YOUR RECENT PAST

THOSE GOOD OLDE DAYS

By Andrea SkyWalker
©1986

OH I LOVE THOSE GOOD OLDE DAYS
REMINDS ME WHEN I WAS MUCH YOUNGER
WE COULD SHARE GOOD TIMES TOGETHER
CAN'T FORGET THOSE GOOD OLDE DAYS

FROM THE MOUNTAINS TO THE STREAMS
THROUGH THE HILLS WE CHASED OUR DREAMS
THEN WE SETTLED BY THE RIVER
AND WE STAYED RIGHT THERE TOGETHER

OH I LOVE THOSE GOOD OLDE DAYS
REMINDS ME WHEN I WAS MUCH YOUNGER
WE COULD SHARE GOOD TIMES TOGETHER
CAN'T FORGET THOSE GOOD OLDE DAYS

"Bottlebrush" by Ru Otto

THOSE INCREDIBLE EYES

By Andrea SkyWalker
©2017

THOSE EYES
THOSE INCREDIBLE EYES
THOSE EYES CONTAIN ALL
THE SECRETS OF THE UNIVERSE
THE PAST - THE FUTURE
AND ALL OF ETERNITY
THOSE EYES ARE INCREDIBLE
THOSE EYES ARE AMAZING
INTOXICATING
THOSE ARE EYES TO GET LOST IN
THE CAVERNS OF THE SOUL
THE DARK AND THE LIGHT
THE EYES OF HAPPINESS
THE EYES OF TEARS
THE LOOK OF GENIUS
THE LOOK OF ENLIGHTENMENT
THOSE INCREDIBLE EYES

"Cougar" by Ru Otto

THROUGH YOUR CHILDREN'S EYES

By Andrea SkyWalker
©2001

THROUGH YOUR CHILDREN'S EYES SHE WATCHES
THE BEAUTY THAT YOU HAVE CREATED
THE EFFORTS THAT YOU HAVE MADE
THE DUES THAT YOU HAVE PAID

THROUGH YOUR CHILDREN'S EYES SHE WATCHES
YOUR TRIALS AND TRIBULATION
AND THEIR AMAZED ELATION
AS THE DREAMS YOU HAVE DREAMED COME TRUE

THROUGH YOUR CHILDREN'S EYES SHE WATCHES
THE PLEASURE - THE PAIN
LOVE'S SWEET REFRAIN
THE SHARED MEMORIES OF TIMES GONE BY

SOME MEMORIES MAY HAVE FADED
MAY BE JADED
BUT THE THINGS YOU HAVE STATED
HAVE COME TO PASS

THROUGH YOUR CHILDREN'S EYES SHE WATCHES
THE APPRECIATION THEY FEEL FOR YOU
THAT YOU CARE
THAT YOU'RE ALWAYS THERE

THROUGH YOUR CHILDREN'S EYES SHE WATCHES

TIME

By Andrea SkyWalker
©1967

WHAT EXISTED ON THIS EARTH
BEFORE PEOPLE
BEFORE PREHISTORIC ANIMALS
BEFORE THE SMALLEST AMOEBA

WHAT WAS THERE
BEFORE THE UNIVERSE
BEFORE GOD
WAS THERE ONE BIG EMPTY SPACE
OF NOTHINGNESS

"Banishing Fundamental Darkness" by Ru Otto

TWO WOUNDED PEOPLE

By Andrea SkyWalker
©2017

TWO WOUNDED PEOPLE
PASSING EACH OTHER
LIKE SHIPS IN THE NIGHT
YOU'RE ALL RIGHT

TWO WOUNDED PEOPLE
SEARCHING FOR A BEACON OF LIGHT
YOU'RE ALL RIGHT

WITH A SLIT OF THE WRIST
AND A TUFFET OF HAIR
THEY SIT ON A DOORSTEP
WITH A LOOK OF DISPAIR
ITS ALL THERE - IT'S ALL THERE

TWO WOUNDED PEOPLE
DECIDING WHETHER TO BE
OR NOT TO BE
THE CHOICE IS THERE
WHETHER TO CARE

TWO WOUNDED PEOPLE
MAKING IT THROUGH ANOTHER NIGHT
WITH A LOOK OF DELIGHT
IT'S ALL RIGHT

TWO WOUNDED PEOPLE
WILL THEY FIND HAPPINESS IN THE AIR
IT'S ALL THERE - WE ALL CARE

WAKE UP

By Andrea SkyWalker
©2017

WAKE UP - WAKE UP - WAKE UP
YOU'VE BEEN SLEEPING FAR TOO LONG
WAKE UP - WAKE UP - WAKE UP
YOU ARE WISE AND YOU ARE STRONG

IT'S TIME TO STAND - IT'S TIME TO STAND
IT'S TIME TO DO WHAT YOU CAN
IT'S TIME TO STAND - IT'S TIME TO STAND
TO BE THE WOMAN AND BE THE MAN

BE KIND - BE KIND - BE KIND
I'LL TAKE YOU BY TH HAND
BE KIND - BE KIND - BE KIND
FOR THE CHILDREN AND THE LAND

WAR

By Andrea SkyWalker
©1967

WAR IS AN EVIL THING
WHICH HATRED BRINGS
WAR IS A FATAL THING
TO WHICH FIGHTING CLINGS
WAR IS A FORCEFUL THING
WHERE NO FREEDOM RINGS
WAR IS A CRUEL THING
WHERE NO CHILDREN SING

"Breakthrough" by Ru Otto

WE ARE LIKE THE LOTUS

By Andrea SkyWalker
©2017

WE ARE LIKE THE LOTUS FLOWER
THAT BLOOMS AND SEEDS IN A MUDDY SWAMP
ONLY TO EMERGE IN BEAUTY
AND FULLY CONSCIOUS
OF THE JOURNEY IT HAD TO ENDURE
TO BECOME WHAT IT IS
THE TRIALS AND TRIBULATIONS
ARE A NECESSITY FOR ITS GROWTH
AND DEVELOPMENT
THE HARSHER THE CLIMATE
THE STRONGER THE CORE
THE HARSHNESS ILLUMINATES THE CORE
WE ARE LIKE THE LOTUS FLOWER
WE'RE ALL OVER THE EARTH

WE STAND TOGETHER

By Andrea SkyWalker
©2017

WE STAND TOGETHER - WE STAND TOGETHER
WE STAND TOGETHER - WE STAND TOGETHER

WE HAVE THE RIGHT TO PRAY TONIGHT
TO PRAY TONIGHT - TILL MORNING LIGHT
IN WIND AND WEATHER - WE STAND TOGETHER

TILL MORNING LIGHT - THE SUN SHINES BRIGHT
IT'S NOW OR NEVER - WE STAND TOGETHER

WE KNOW THE TRUTH OF WHICH WE SPEAK
WE STAND TOGETHER - OUT IN THE STREET

IN WIND AND WEATHER
IF WE STAND TOGETHER
THERE SHALL BE PEACE
THERE SHALL BE PEACE

WE'RE READY TO FIGHT

By Andrea SkyWalker
©1980

WE'RE READY TO FIGHT
WE'RE GONNA UNITE
ONWARD TO VICORY
WITH SMILES
BRIGHT AS THE SHINING SUN
WE'LL WIN THE FIGHT
FOR PEACE BECAUSE IT'S RIGHT
WORLD PEACE IS SURE TO COME

COME JOIN US TONIGHT
WE'RE READY TO FIGHT
ONWARD TO VICTORY
WITH LIGHT
FROM THE MOON ABOVE
WE'LL DO OUR PART
WE KNOW THAT DIALOGUE'S THE START
THE WORLD WILL BE AS ONE

WHAT IF YOU LEAVE

By Andrea SkyWalker
©2001

WHAT AM I GOING TO DO IF YOU LEAVE
I FINALLY GOT YOU HERE
NOW YOU WANNA LEAVE

CRYING ON MY SLEEVE
I CAN'T BELIEVE
YOU ALREADY WANNA LEAVE

PLEASE STAY - DON'T GO AWAY
I WANT TO LOVE YOU ANOTHER DAY

I FEEL YOUR SOUL
YOU DON'T HAVE TO LIE
DON'T JUST GIVE UP AND DIE

THERE'S NO TIME FOR DOWN TIME
THERE'S JUST TIME FOR TIME
THERE'S NO TIME BUT OUR TIME
LET'S MAKE TIME FOR TIME

WHEN I LOOK INTO YOUR EYES

By Andrea SkyWalker
©2017

WHEN I LOOK INTO YOUR EYES
I CAN SEE GOD - THE UNIVERSE
AND ALL OF CREATION

I SEE THE PLAYFUL
I SEE THE SERIOUS
I SEE THE GROWTH
I SEE THE WISDOM
THERE IS NO ENEMY

I SEE THE GOOD
I SEE THE BEST
I SEE THE GENIUS
I SEE THE MIND

IT'S NOT THE FLESH
IT'S NOT THE BLOOD
IT'S NOT THE FORM

IT'S BEHIND
BEYOND THE EYES
IT'S THE GLORY
IT'S THE PROFUNDITY
IT PERMEATES THE UNIVERSE
THE TRAGEDY - THE COMEDY - THE DRAMA
I SEE IT ALL

WHEN YOU THINK OF ME

By Andrea SkyWalker
©2001

WHEN YOU THINK OF ME
I KNOW IT
WHEN YOU THINK OF ME
AND I THINK OF YOU
I LIKE IT
I TAKE IT AS IT IS
FOR WHAT IT'S WORTH
IN THE MOMENT
AND LET IT SINK IN

"Comedy of Eros" by Ru Otto

WHO CARES

By Andrea SkyWalker
©2017

ILLEGAL IMMIGRANTS - DROWNING
WHO CARES
ILLITERATE CAJUNS - DROWNING
WHO CARES
FORMER AFRICAN SLAVES - DROWNING
WHO CARES
ANGRY PITBULLS - DROWNING
WHO CARES
WELL-EDUCATED CAUCASIANS
IN UPPER-CLASS NEIGHBORHOODS
DROWNING
WHO CARES
INNOCENT BABIES CRYING TO BE SAVED
DROWNING
WHO CARES
CITIZENS OF THE EARTH - DROWNING
WHO CARES

WHY HATE

by Andrea SkyWalker
©1967

WHY DO PEOPLE HATE THE ONES THEY SHOULD LOVE
WHY DO THEY THINK THEY ARE SO HIGH ABOVE
JUST BECAUSE A PEOPLE'S SKIN IS BLACK
WHY DO THE OTHERS HAVE TO TURN THEIR BACK
WHO IN THIS WORLD HAS THE RIGHT TO SHUN
GOD MADE THIS WORLD FOR EVERYONE
THIS WORLD SHOULD BE FOR LOVE AND PLAY
AND OF COURSE A BIT OF WORK EACH DAY
BUT NOT FOR BUILDING BOMBS TO KILL
THIS IS NOT IN GOD'S WILL

"In the Pink" by Janie Whited

WONDER IN THE AIR

by Andrea SkyWalker
©2016

THE ROSES BLOOM IN A BOUQUET
OF OTHER FLOWERS
WHICH ARE NO LESS BEAUTIFUL
OR IMPORTANT
BECAUSE THEY ALL MATTER EQUALLY
THE SCENT IS HEAVENLY
SENDING FRAGRANCE
THROUGHOUT THE HOUSE
THE OTHERS ARE MIXED
IN COLOR AND VARIETY
ENHANCING THE BEAUTY OF THE ROSES
THE VASE IS GLOWING RED
ILLUMINATING THE ROOM
AND THE PERSON WATCHING
THIS MIRACLE UNFOLD
NEXT TO THE BOUQUET
SITS A BOX OF SWEET CHOCOLATES
AND A CARD DECLARING UNDYING LOVE
FOR THE RECIPIENT
THERE IS WONDER IN THE AIR

WORDS

By Andrea SkyWalker
©2006

THE WORDS THEY COME
LIKE BULLETS FROM A GUN
THE WORDS THEY COME ARUNNIN'

THE WORDS THEY FLOW LIKE RAIN INTO SNOW
IN THE SUN THEY WILL GLOW
THE WORDS THEY COME ARUNNIN'

THE WORDS THEY HURT
THEY COME FROM DIRT
THE WORDS THEY COME ARUNNIN'

THE WORDS THEY SHINE
THEY FLOW LIKE WINE
FROM YOUR HEART TO MINE
THE WORDS THEY COME ARUNNIN'

YOU SAID

By Andrea SkyWalker
©2001

YOU'VE BEEN GONE AN ETERNITY
YOU SAID YOU'D NEVER LEAVE
YOU LIED
I'VE CRIED A MILLION TIMES
I'D WALK A MILLION MILES FOR YOU
YOU SAID YOU LOVED AND WANTED ME
JUST ME
YOU SAID AND I BELIEVED
I FELL FOR YOU
YOU SAID YOU'D NEVER LEAVE
AND I BELIEVED IN YOU
YOU SAID
YOU MUST HAVE LIED A MILLION TIMES BEFORE
BUT YOU SAID
AND I BELIEVED IN YOU

"Ride the Waves" by Ru Otto

YOU

By Andrea SkyWalker
©2001

YOU INFLUENCED MY LIFE
IN A POSITIVE WAY
WHEN I THOUGHT I COULDN'T GO ON

THANK YOU - THANK YOU

YOU INFLUENCED MY LIFE
IN A POSITIVE WAY
WHEN I COULDN'T SLEEP TILL DAWN

THANK YOU - THANK YOU

YOU WOKE ME UP TO THE LIGHT OF THE DAY
WHEN ALL WAS DARK AND GRAY

THANK YOU - THANK YOU

YOU WOKE ME UP TO THE BEAUTY OF LIFE
BY TEACHING ME HOW TO APPRECIATE
THE VALUE OF FRIENDS

THANK YOU - THANK YOU

YOU'RE STILL YOU

By Andrea SkyWalker
©2001

THROUGH THE DARKNESS
I CAN SEE YOUR LIGHT
AND YOU WILL ALWAYS SHINE
AND I CAN FEEL YOUR HEART IN MINE

YOUR FACE I'VE MEMORIZED
I IDOLIZE JUST YOU
I LOOK UP TO EVERYTHING YOU ARE
IN MY EYES YOU DO NO WRONG
I'VE LOVED YOU FOR SO LONG
AND AFTER ALL IS SAID AND DONE
YOU'RE STILL YOU
AFTER ALL

YOU'RE STILL YOU
YOU WALK PAST ME
I CAN FEEL YOUR PAIN
TIME CHANGES EVERYTHING
ONE TRUTH ALWAYS STAYS THE SAME
YOU'RE STILL YOU
AFTER ALL
YOU'RE STILL YOU

I LOOK UP TO EVERYTHING YOU ARE
IN MY EYES YOU DO NO WRONG
AND I BELIEVE IN YOU
ALTHOUGH YOU NEVER ASK ME TO
I WILL REMEMBER YOU
AND WHAT LIFE PUT YOU THROUGH

AND IN THIS CRUEL AND LONELY WORLD
I FOUND ONE LOVE
YOU'RE STILL YOU
AFTER ALL
YOU'RE STILL YOU

"Butterfly on a Daisy" by Janie Whited

TO
MY LOVELY
LIFE LONG FRIEND
LORRIE-
ENJOY.

Andrea SkyWalker

See P. 76

62321474R00077

Made in the USA
Columbia, SC
01 July 2019